Frank Richard Stockton

The Watchmaker's Wife

And Other Stories

Frank Richard Stockton

The Watchmaker's Wife
And Other Stories

ISBN/EAN: 9783337004705

Printed in Europe, USA, Canada, Australia, Japan

Cover: Foto ©Thomas Meinert / pixelio.de

More available books at **www.hansebooks.com**

THE WATCHMAKER'S WIFE

AND

OTHER STORIES

FRANK R. STOCKTON'S WRITINGS.

New Uniform Edition.

THE RUDDER GRANGERS ABROAD, and Other Stories.
THE BEE-MAN OF ORN, and Other Fanciful Tales.
THE LADY, OR THE TIGER? and Other Stories.
THE CHRISTMAS WRECK, and Other Stories.
AMOS KILBRIGHT, and Other Stories.
THE LATE MRS. NULL.
RUDDER GRANGE.

*** *The set, seven vols.*, $8.75; *each*, $1.25.

RUDDER GRANGE. *New Illustrated Edition.* With over 100 Illustrations by A. B. FROST. Square 12mo, $2.00.

THE RUDDER GRANGERS ABROAD, and Other Stories. 12mo, paper, 50 cents.

THE LADY, OR THE TIGER? and Other Stories. 12mo, paper, 50 cents.

THE CHRISTMAS WRECK, and Other Stories. 12mo, paper, 50 cents.

RUDDER GRANGE. 12mo, paper, 60 cents.

AMOS KILBRIGHT. 12mo, paper, 50 cents.

A JOLLY FELLOWSHIP. Illustrated, 12mo, $1.50.

THE STORY OF VITEAU. Illustrated, 12mo, $1.50.

THE TING-A-LING TALES. Illustrated, 12mo, $1.00.

THE FLOATING PRINCE, and Other Fairy Tales. Illustrated, 4to, cloth, $1.50.

ROUNDABOUT RAMBLES IN LANDS OF FACT AND FANCY. Illustrated, 4to, boards, $1.50.

TALES OUT OF SCHOOL. Illustrated, 4to, boards, $1.50.

PERSONALLY CONDUCTED. Illustrated, square 8vo, $2.00.

THE WATCHMAKER'S WIFE

AND

OTHER STORIES

BY

FRANK R. STOCKTON

NEW YORK
CHARLES SCRIBNER'S SONS
1893

CONTENTS

THE WATCHMAKER'S WIFE

IT was late on a quiet August afternoon that the little yacht "Flippant" sailed into the harbor of a small New England town. The yacht, which was a very small one, belonged to my friend, George Crimrose, who had invited me to take a week's cruise with him along the coast. There was no one on board but our two selves, and, in fact, there was neither room nor need for anybody else. Crimrose generally sat at the helm, while I acted the part of a crew and steward. Crimrose cooked our meals.

"If General Washington were aboard," he had remarked, "I might let him attend to the sails and anchor, but I should want to do the cooking myself."

We had been out four days and were now bound homeward, and after passing the night in the quiet harbor we proposed to start on our southerly course to Boston. Crimrose had intended going on shore to put a letter in the post-office; but as it was past supper-time before we entered the harbor, he concluded to postpone this until morning. We had no small boat but the yacht, which was sloop-rigged, and was so small that we could easily run her up to a pier, or even ground her on a beach. Our sails had been lowered, anchor dropped, supper cooked and eaten, and pipes smoked; we hung out our lantern and retired to rest. The "Flippant" was really nothing more than a sail-boat, though Crimrose always insisted in calling her a yacht. But there was a little deck cabin divided into two parts, each of which was large enough to satisfy the needs of a tired man. There was a slight breeze from the southeast, and the gentle rising and falling of the boat soon lulled us to sleep.

When I awoke the next morning I knew it must be a fine day, because I could see through the opening of the curtains which hung at the entrance of my little cabin the early sunlight upon the water, and I concluded that there could not be any wind at all at present, for the little vessel was perfectly motionless, and I could not feel the slightest swell nor movement of the water. This was unfortunate, because if we were to reach Boston at the time we expected, we should need a good wind that day.

I got up and dressed myself, and went on deck. It was indeed a beautiful day and a quiet one, and looking out over the stern I was surprised to see, instead of the town or the sand-hills in the sides of its little harbor, a wide expanse of water on which there was a slight but well-defined swell. Turning to look behind me, I stood utterly astounded — the yacht was ashore, one-half her length lying on a sandy beach. No wonder I did not feel the movement of the sea.

For nearly a minute I stood gazing about me in amazement. Before me was a wide beach; back of that a higher bit of land sprinkled with rocks and coarse shore-grass, and still farther back, a wood, principally of pines, which shut out the view beyond. This wood extended for a considerable distance to the right and left and then there was the sea again.

Crimrose was a heavy sleeper, and I could still hear his deep breathing. Before awakening him I determined to make some further investigation, and quietly walking forward, I stepped ashore. As I did this I fancied the vessel made a little movement forward, but this I attributed to my excited state of mind. I walked around the bow of the vessel, and the longer I looked at her, the more I was puzzled and astonished at her situation. She was not only grounded, but her forepart was deep in the soft sand. How this could have happened I could not conceive. Had she broken from her anchorage and drifted upon this point of land, or island, or whatever it was, she would have grounded broadside to the beach, and perhaps stern foremost; but how she could have gone ashore head on, and with such force as to drive her so deeply into the sand that she stood on her even keel, and all this without shock enough to wake either of us, passed my comprehension. I wanted to think it out before I woke Crimrose, who was such a quick and impulsive man, and so full of reasons for everything that could possibly happen, that he disturbed my methods of quiet ratiocination. I would wait a little, and endeavor to work out the problem myself. As I stood gazing at the vessel, my eyes fell upon the boom near where it was attached to the lower part of the mast, and there, closely pressing the boom and the furled sail, I saw a crooked piece of iron which I had never noticed before. This was attached to a stout rope which ran upward along the mast, making one or two turns around it. My eyes followed this rope upward to the masthead, and then above the masthead, and on up, higher and higher, and then throwing my head backward, my eyes followed the rope still higher and higher until it ended at a balloon in the air above me.

There was but little wind; the balloon was almost stationary, and was apparently not much more than a hundred feet above the ground. From the wicker car which hung beneath it there came no sign of occupancy. I ran along the beach a little way that I might better look up without stretching my neck, and then I sat down on the beach and quietly laughed to myself. Here was an unheard-of and ridiculous situation, and I was delighted that I had fully investigated and worked out the whole problem before waking Crimrose.

The condition was now easy enough to understand; the dangling grappling-iron of an escaped balloon had caught in the boom of the "Flippant"; with a gentle breeze, which was probably blowing early in the night, the strain at first was very slight, but this strain was continuous and strong, and our cable had parted or our anchor had dragged, and we had been towed bow foremost by the balloon until we had touched this beach, and then slowly and steadily had been drawn forward until the bow of the vessel was so deep in the sand that the balloon could move it no further, and here we were. Now I would awaken Crimrose.

This experienced navigator was not half dressed before he perceived that his yacht was unnaturally motionless, and it was not two seconds after he had put his head out from between his little curtains that he was on deck gazing wildly about him. In another second, bareheaded and barefooted, he had sprung upon the sand, and stood by my side. At that instant the "Flippant," before our eyes, moved forward a foot, it seemed to me. This was easy enough to understand; Crimrose was tall, and round, and plump, and stepping ashore he relieved the craft of more than two hundred pounds of weight.

I pointed into the air, and glancing upward, Crimrose saw the balloon. When he appreciated the fact that this great object hovering above us was made fast by a long rope to the yacht, Crimrose's lower jaw fell so that it looked as if it were going to drop off, and with eyes like billiard balls he began to feel wildly in his pockets; then he turned to me and gasped: —

"Give me your knife! Cut that rope."

But my mind had been hard at work on the subject of this balloon.

"Don't you do that," I said; "there may be somebody in that car, dead or alive, and if there has been an accident, there may be papers or something. We should not let it blow out to sea and be lost forever."

"What is all that to me?" exclaimed Crimrose, red in the face; "it will have the mast out of my yacht in a minute; it will work her seams loose; it will ruin her. Where is your knife? I have lost mine."

"Crimrose," said I, "if you cut that rope and let that balloon get away, we may do a great injury. Balloons don't float about that way unless something has happened. It won't hurt the 'Flippant' to hold it a little longer, until we make up our minds what is best to do."

"It is best to cut her loose!" exclaimed Crimrose; "that is what we should do."

I put my hand upon his arm.

"Stop," said I; "we can do better than that. First, let us find out whether there is anybody in that car."

Without answering, Crimrose stepped back, put a hand on each side of his mouth, and shouted in a high, shrill voice: —

"Hello, up there!"

Almost immediately a large felt hat appeared above the edge of the basket, and after it a face. It was that of a man with grizzled whiskers and beard.

"Who are you, and what are you about?" shouted Crimrose.

The man put his head a little way over the edge of the basket; he seemed very much afraid of falling out.

"Glad to see you," he shouted; "is that rope hitched tight and strong?"

"Yes," I answered; "you are secure for the present."

"But you can't hook on to my boat any longer," cried Crimrose. "Do you want to come down? If you do, pull your valve-rope and let out your gas."

"I do want to come down," cried the man. "Nobody ever wanted to come down as much as I do, but the valve-rope is broken. I did let out a great deal of the gas, but I can't let out any more now. But don't you think you can get this balloon to the ground? Can't you pull us down?"

"I can bring you down," cried Crimrose; "I will get

my rifle and put some holes in the top of the balloon, and that will let out the gas quick enough!"

I expostulated. "Don't do that," I said; "you might rip a great rent in the silk, so that the balloon would fall suddenly, and the man be killed."

I also thought it likely that in his excitement Crimrose might hit the man in the car instead of the top of the balloon, but I did not think it wise to say this. It was plain to see that a large portion of the gas had escaped, for the lower part of the balloon hung loose and flabby, and the gas that remained was not much more than enough to sustain the occupant of the car at his present moderate distance above the earth. I thought it not at all impossible that we might be able to pull down the balloon.

At a short distance from us, at the edge of the higher ground above the beach, stood a small gnarled tree, cedar or something of the kind, with one of its crooked roots making a little loop above the ground. This, I believed, would be strong enough to hold the balloon, and in a minute I formed a plan.

Crimrose had gone on board to put on his shoes, and while he was doing this I got out a long rope which had been stowed away on the yacht, and making it fast to the grapnel of the balloon, I carried the other end of it to the gnarled tree, passed it under the root, and fastened it to the trunk. By this time Crimrose had reappeared, and I proposed my plan to him.

"All right," said he; "anything so we get her loose from the yacht." And standing on our forward deck, he reached up as far as possible, and took hold of the balloon rope, and hung upon it with his whole weight.

Down came the balloon until Crimrose was on his knees.

"Hurrah!" I cried, and loosening the grapnel from the boom, I ran to the tree, and pulled the rope nearly taut.

"Let go!" I cried, and Crimrose released his hold; the balloon rose into the air, moved over the little tree, and then stopped. With the rope under the root, and a half-turn around the trunk, I found I could easily hold it. Even when the balloon shot upward, there was no cry from the car. Its occupant evidently saw what we were about.

Crimrose was so delighted to see his yacht relieved from the strain of the balloon, that he seemed satisfied with what had been done, and prepared to examine his vessel to discover what damage, if any, it had sustained; but I shouted to him to come to me.

"You pull her down a few feet at a time, and I will keep the rope tight as it shortens; then we shall soon have that man on solid ground."

Crimrose looked up, shook his head a little, but set to work with such vigor that it was not long before the bottom of the car was but a little above the top of the tree. I now saw that the tree branches would interfere with the safe descent of the aeronaut, and making the rope fast to the root, I suggested to Crimrose that he sit down and take a little rest. I then got an axe from the yacht, and cut off the tree not far from the ground; its roots were all that we needed.

Crimrose and I dragged away the little tree, and then we set to work again. When the car was within a few feet of the ground, I cautioned the old man, who gazed at us with an expression which indicated more interest in our proceedings than any other emotion, not to try to get out until I told him to, for the balloon might give a jump and jerk the rope away from us.

"Oh, don't you be afraid," said the man; "I am not going to get out until everything is tight and fast."

When the car was as low as we could get it, and everything was tight and fast, the aeronaut, with much nimbleness, scrambled over the edge of the basket and approached us, offering each a hand.

"Thanks, both of you, ever so much," he said; "if there is ever anything I can do for you, I hope you will let me know."

"How did this happen?" asked Crimrose. "What made you hook on to my yacht?"

"Excuse me one minute, gentlemen," said the man, and going to the basket he put his head over the edge, and looked down into it.

"Come, Sarah," he said; "you can get out now."

At this we were treated to a new surprise; for an elderly woman, wearing a black bonnet, and wrapped in a gray shawl, put her head and shoulders above the side of the car.

"I don't see any steps," she said. "How do people get out of these things?"

"The best way they can, my dear," replied the man; "at least, in a case like this."

"All right," said the old lady, and in a minute she was standing alongside the man.

"This is my wife, gentlemen," said he,—"Mrs. Pocock, and she is just as much obliged to you as I am for helping us to land."

They were a queer-looking couple; the man was short and wiry in build, with twinkling blue eyes, and a line of gray beard under his chin; his wife, shorter than he, with her black bonnet, her spectacles, and gray shawl, looked as little like an aeronaut as could possibly be imagined.

"Indeed I am obliged," said she; "for the last sixteen hours I have been about as much scared as anybody can be, except when I was asleep. And looking over the edge of that car made me so dizzy that I have been curled up in the bottom until I can scarcely get my joints out straight again."

"But how did this all happen?" I asked. "It seems a very odd thing for you two to go up in a balloon."

"Odd! I should say so," replied the man. "I'll tell you in twenty words just how it happened. But by the way, my dear," he interpolated, taking out his watch, "it is not sixteen hours that we have been in the car, for we were thirty minutes late in starting. You see," said he, "I am a watchmaker, Sylvester Pocock, of Barnville, Massachusetts, and for a long time I have wanted to test the movements of a watch at different altitudes. Great things might come out of experiments of this kind. At last I got a chance; I made the acquaintance of an aeronaut, and he agreed to take me up with him."

"And me," added Mrs. Pocock; "for I would not let my husband go alone."

"He wanted three persons," continued the watchmaker, "and as Mrs. Pocock might never have such a chance again, I agreed to take her."

"Put it as you please," his wife remarked, "anyway I went."

"Well, gentlemen," continued the watchmaker, "you may scarcely believe it, but I tell you that after me and Mrs. Pocock had snugly packed ourselves in that car, me with three of my best watches in my pockets, and she with everything to make her comfortable for an hour's sail, which was all we bargained for, that aeronaut — a large man by the way, and a little given, I am afraid, to ardent spirits — actually fell out of his balloon just as the rope had been cut. He was waving his hat and leaning far over the edge of the car, and I think made a grab at something somebody held out to him, when out he toppled, turned a somersault, and came down on his feet, and at that instant up we went with a shoot that nearly took our breath away. I don't believe he was hurt much, for I could see him running and waving his arms, and then in a short time everything seemed to be fading away, and we went on, up and up, scarcely knowing what had happened."

"Scarcely!" said Mrs. Pocock; "as far as I was concerned, it wasn't as much as that. I knew nothing at all except that that man had tumbled over the edge of the car, and it made me so dizzy even to think of looking over that I curled myself up in the bottom, as I told you, knowing no more about anything than if I hadn't been there."

"I did what I could," said the watchmaker; "but that wasn't much. I knew if I let out the gas, the balloon would come down, so I got hold of the valve-rope and let out a lot of the gas, and we came down pretty fast. Then I began to think we were coming down too fast, and I let the valve shut again. At that time we were not much further from the ground than when we were fastened to your boat, and the wind was taking us along slowly. I could see people below, and a good many of them shouted to us. I tried to open the valve again, thinking we'd let ourselves down kind of gradual, when the rope broke, and that was the end of it. The wind took us along, we not knowing what to do, and at last I thought of letting out the grappling-iron, and then I did it as quick as I could, but it wasn't no use. We passed over fences and trees and lots of things it might have caught onto; but our rope didn't reach low enough, and we went on and on until it got dark and couldn't see things below us, and as there wasn't anything else to be done, I thought I might as well try to make myself comfortable and take a nap, for when daylight came I might need all the strength I'd got. The fact is, I didn't wake up until I heard you calling to me. Sometime in the night I felt a little sort of a jerk which must have been when we hooked onto your boat, but I didn't know what it was, and I didn't get up to look out; for, to tell the truth, it was a dreadful thing, peering out over the top of that basket into the blackness of the night. I think it likely when the night drew on, the balloon sunk more and more until the grappling-iron got low enough to catch onto your boat, which was a blessed thing for us, gentlemen, for where we'd drifted to if we hadn't hooked fast to you, there's no telling."

"But all's well that ends well," said Crimrose; "and now let us have some breakfast. I suppose you must be hungry; at any rate, I am."

"Now that my feet's on the ground, I am hungry," said Mrs. Pocock; "for it was in the afternoon when we went up, and we expected to come down again in plenty of time for supper."

While Crimrose, assisted by Mrs. Pocock and the watchmaker, prepared the morning meal, I started off to find out, if possible, where we were. I walked along the beach to the eastward and soon finding myself at the end of the little woods, I went inland and scrambled to the top of a rocky hill, and from this I could plainly see that we were on one of the small uninhabited islands which dot the coast of New England.

At varying distances, but none of them nearer than half a mile, were other islands — I counted five of them altogether. When I made this discovery, I went back to the beach and found breakfast ready. The meal was a very good one. Mrs. Pocock, who evidently was a woman who was in the habit of having her own way, had done a good many things in the way of cooking which Crimrose generally insisted on doing himself. We all began in pleasant humor to discuss the situation.

"I don't know what island this is," said Crimrose, "but, from my knowledge of the coast, I am quite sure that if we take a southwesterly course we shall soon be in sight of land, and then I shall have my bearings. I shall be glad to take you two to Boston with us, and then you can easily go to your home by train."

"But how about the balloon? How are we going to get that back to Barnville?" asked the watchmaker.

Crimrose laughed. "The best thing we can do with

the balloon is to get your traps out of her and cut her loose and let her sail to the north pole, and it might be a good idea to put our names on a card in it, and then perhaps in that way at least we might get ahead of any Arctic explorers. I should like the men who finally discover the north pole to find my name there."

"That is a pleasant fancy," said Mr. Pocock, "but it will not do. Robert Moxham, who owns the balloon, can't afford to lose her; and after his kindness in agreeing to take me up to make my experiments, it would be a pretty mean thing for me to go away and leave his property if there was any way of getting it back to him. I reckon that if we was to cut some slits in the bag that could easily be sewed up again, that would let out the gas, we could pack up the balloon and take it along. Of course we should have to leave the car behind, for that would be most too big for your boat."

"Well," said Crimrose, "if you can do all that before I am ready to sail, I don't mind, but I can't wait for you. I've got to be in Boston to-morrow night, which is Saturday, for I have very important business on hand next week. The fact is, I am to be married, and this is my last bachelor cruise."

"Married!" exclaimed Mrs. Pocock, taking off her spectacles and looking at him; "that is very interesting."

"Yes, and to the best girl in the world. And now let us go and get the 'Flippant' afloat. There will be a good wind in half an hour, or I am no sailor."

We had spread the breakfast cloth upon the clean

sand, and Mrs. Pocock now began to gather up the dishes, while Crimrose walked to the yacht. The tide had already risen, and the little boat was now almost surrounded by water. The watchmaker went toward the balloon, with a troubled expression; he would require a good deal of help before he could pull it down low enough to cut a split in the upper part, and then it would take a good while to pack it.

I stood looking out over the sea. For the time I forgot the strange chance by which we had been towed by a balloon to this island; the unexpected arrival from the upper air of an addition to our party, and the work to be done in order that we might get afloat and start on our homeward cruise; all was forgotten in the thought that next week Crimrose was to be married to the girl I loved.

The story of my affections can be told in a few words: I had loved Jeannette Collins for a long time, and I had a fancy she knew it, but was not sure, for I had never told her. Often and often had I intended to tell her, but there had always been some reason why I had deferred speaking. In those days I was not a man who always acted with the promptness that his interests demanded.

But when Crimrose arrived upon the scene during the previous winter, he proved to be a man of unusual promptness. Without any hesitation at all he fell in love with Jeannette, and very shortly afterward offered himself to her. I have reason to know that the matter was not settled immediately. But after a time it was settled, and they were to be married next week. It had not been generally expected that the marriage would take place so soon; but Crimrose had determined upon a wedding trip to Europe, and his plans demanded that this should be begun before the summer was over. As I said before, he was very prompt and energetic in everything that he did.

But it was of no use to think of those things then. I had shut my lips tightly, and ground my teeth pretty often during the last six months, and I did it again. Then I went to the yacht to help Crimrose get it afloat. We found this not so easy a task as we supposed it would be. Though Mr. Pocock added his strength to ours, we were not able to push the "Flippant" back into the water in which her stern was already afloat. During our efforts the tide rose considerably higher, and then we were surprised to see that the bow of the yacht did not rise with it.

"By George!" cried Crimrose, "I believe the water is running into her instead of lifting her." And on examination this was found to be true; the "Flippant" was leaking forward. We now all set to work to keel over the yacht, and before long we discovered the damage and the cause of it. A jagged bit of rock, nearly buried in the sand, had been pressed against her bottom by the steady strain of the balloon, until it made a hole a foot and a half long.

This was to us all a doleful sight. Even Mrs. Pocock could appreciate the extent of the disaster. The "Flippant" was an old boat, although Crimrose had always asserted that she was just as good as if she had been built the day before, and I fancy her planks were rotten, for the piece of rock had broken through her bottom as if it had been made of earthenware. Even while we were examining the lamentable fracture, the water was gradually rising and concealing it from our view, and we could not keel over the "Flippant" any farther.

Crimrose, who had been standing half-leg deep in water, now splashed ashore and began to clench his fists and swear.

"Do you know," he shouted to me, "that we can't leave this island? It is impossible for us to repair that yacht, and in twenty minutes she will be full of water." And turning toward the balloon, he addressed it in terms which, had the great swaying body had ears, would have dreadfully shocked it. As it was, it shocked Mr. and Mrs. Pocock.

"I am very sorry," said the watchmaker, "that that balloon should have caused your disaster; but for all that I am glad our grapnel caught in your yacht. If it had not, my wife and I might have floated out to sea and been forever lost. As it is, we are all four on dry land."

"Dry land!" exclaimed Crimrose; "I don't want to be on dry land. I am on my way to Boston, and how in the name of all that's wicked am I to get there?"

"Perhaps some passing vessel may take us off," suggested Mrs. Pocock, quietly.

"Passing vessel!" returned Crimrose; "when vessels pass, they don't pass anywhere near such a villanous bunch of rocks as this. Confound that balloon! Somebody give me a knife."

The watchmaker rose to the occasion. "There's no use in getting angry, sir," said he, "and it won't help matters to cut loose the balloon. If there is anything to eat and drink on board your boat, and if there is any property there that you wish to keep from getting wet, I think we ought to wade in and bring it ashore."

"The most sensible thing that has been said yet," said Mrs. Pocock to me, and I agreed with her.

In half an hour everything that could be moved from the yacht had been brought ashore and been carried up to the sheltered spot near the wood, and Crimrose was sitting on a rock with his fingers in his hair.

"I tell you," he cried, "there was never anything so diabolically unlucky since the beginning of the world. It may be hours and even a day before a fishing-boat or any other craft comes near this wretched island. And what am I to do? I did not even mail my letter to Jeannette last night. She hasn't heard from me since we started, and if I am not home to-morrow, she will be certain to think I am drowned. It will kill her. Yes, sir! It will kill her."

Mrs. Pocock, who was not far away, was much affected by this view of the case. Drawing me aside, she said: —

"It seems to me, sir, that this is a pretty bad state of things. As far as living goes, there is nothing much to complain of, and the weather's mild, and we have victuals enough to last us for a week if we are careful. But when we think there is a poor lady on shore expecting to be married early next week and having every reason to believe that her intended is at the bottom of the sea, it is enough to make anybody's heart ache. Do you know the young lady, sir? I think you must, for you are looking awfully doleful yourself. Is she of a tender disposition?"

I was indeed feeling very doleful, and I was glad to have the opportunity of speaking to one so sympathetic as this good woman. I described Jeannette to her in a way that made her look very steadfastly at me.

"It is a great pity that a woman like that should be weeping for a lost lover, and he safe on this dry land. Have you known the lady long, sir?" she asked. "I suppose your friend was proud to make you acquainted with such a lady."

"Make me acquainted!" I exclaimed; "I have known her for years, and he never saw her until last Christmas."

"I am a person who speaks her mind," said she, after another steadfast gaze at me, "and if the young woman is all you say she is, it strikes me that it is a pity that somebody else did not marry her before that other gentleman met her."

"What do you mean by that?" I said quickly.

"The principal thing I mean," said she, "is that I don't think much of him. But I dare say you consider I have no right to meddle in affairs that don't concern me, and so I'll stop it."

I looked in astonishment at the watchmaker's wife; she was certainly a person who meddled with matters that were none of her business.

The greater part of the day was passed in vain efforts to discover some approaching vessel. We hoisted our flag upside down on the mast of the yacht; we hung a sheet from the tallest tree on the edge of the wood; but the day began to close, and we saw no sign of life upon the water except the smoke of some distant steamers. The sun was already low when Crimrose came hurrying to me with Mr. Pocock.

"This man," said he, "has proposed something which may be of service. He has noticed, and I should have noticed it myself if my mind had not been so disturbed, that the wind has veered to the southeast, and says that that balloon of his will easily carry one person, and that if one of us were to get in her and put the valve in working order, it would not take long for this breeze to blow the balloon to the mainland. It would be easy enough then to come down and send somebody over here to take us off. If word could be sent immediately to Jeannette, and I could get home by Sunday, things would not be so very bad, after all."

"That's a good idea," said the watchmaker's wife, "and I wonder none of us thought of it before."

"It was of no use thinking of it," said her husband, "until the wind changed."

"Then I suppose the thing ought to be done as soon as may be before the wind changes again," said she. "I should say, Mr. Crimrose, that when you go over, you'll have to leave the balloon wherever you land, to stay there until it is called for, and then you will send some sort of a vessel here to take us off."

"Me!" exclaimed Crimrose; "I can't go in the balloon. I am ever so much too heavy. She wouldn't begin to carry me."

"I don't believe you weigh any more than me and Mr. Pocock," said she.

"I think I do," said Crimrose; "besides, there isn't as much gas in the balloon as when you came down.

Of course it is always escaping. But there is plenty to carry a light person, say Mr. Pocock, and he understands more about balloons than I do, anyway."

"Mr. Pocock!" exclaimed the watchmaker's wife; "I would like you to know, sir, that Mr. Pocock weighs just as much as he and me weighs; for if he goes, I go, for he don't go without me. And when I say that there is nothing on earth that would tempt me to get into a balloon again,—for sooner than do that I'd spend the rest of my life here, at least as long as roots and leaves and fish, if we could get any, would keep me alive, —you will understand that Mr. Pocock is not going in that balloon. It is so important that you should get over to the mainland just as soon as you can, and as it doesn't matter to the rest of us if we wait here awhile until we can be taken off comfortably, I should say that you are the man who ought to go, and I believe the balloon would carry you just as well as not. Mr. Pocock and I is short, but we're solid."

Crimrose put his hands in his pockets and walked toward the beach.

"That wouldn't do at all," he said; "a light person would be perfectly safe, but it wouldn't carry me."

I put my hands in my pockets and walked toward the beach. There was no disguising the fact that I was a light person,— at least, a great deal lighter than Crimrose. The next day was Saturday. Fishing-vessels seldom started out on Saturday, and it was not likely that any small craft would be sailing as far as this against a rising east wind. Even now Jeannette must be feeling a great deal of anxiety; for Crimrose had told her that he might possibly be back by Friday, although I had not thought there was any reason for supposing he would be able to do this. Moreover, he had not sent her the letter, which I certainly should have found an opportunity to mail had I been in his place. Even if she had been sure he was safe, the case was a very bad one; for if Crimrose did not get back before Monday or Tuesday, the wedding would have to be postponed, and I could imagine how Jeannette would feel if her wedding did not take place on the day for which all the preparations had been made. Crimrose should never have started on a cruise like this at such a time. I had told him so; but he was a man who would have his own way, and I am not at all sure that the desire to get him back in good time had not assisted me to make up my mind to go with him. I stood and looked out over the water, and then I turned to Crimrose, who was also meditating.

"I think I will go over in that balloon," I said.

He sprang toward me, his face blazing with delight. "Harry," he cried, seizing one of my hands in both of his, "you are a trump! You are a friend indeed, and it is just what I should have expected from you. The thing is easy enough to do, of course, and I should be the first man to offer to go if the balloon were filled with gas; but it won't carry me as it is, and it will carry you; and although I should not have asked you to do it, I accept your offer with all the gratitude that one friend can show another."

"Come on," said I; "let us get the balloon in shape to start; that valve should be put in order."

Crimrose was full of enthusiasm. "I am very sure there is nothing the matter with the valve, except that the cord is broken. If we tie another piece of string to it, you will be all right, and have as much command of the balloon as if you were driving a pony to a cart. I will get some cord and make that right in no time."

Mr. Pocock came to me.

"I didn't think you'd be the one to go," said he, "but that is not my affair. But I believe the balloon will carry you; and if you take all the rope you can get off of that boat and make the grappling-line longer, I haven't a doubt you can catch hold of something as soon as you get over land."

The watchmaker's wife came and stood close by me.

"Well, well," said she, "you must have a powerful friendship for that gentleman to undertake such a trip for him. You couldn't do more if he was your own brother,— but perhaps you were boys together?"

"Oh no," said I, "I haven't known him long, and I can't say it is for his sake I am going." I did not intend to make this remark, but it came out very naturally.

"Oh!" said she, "it isn't, isn't it? Well, it is a bad thing for a young lady expecting to be married not to know what's become of her intended, and perhaps not to see him turn up until the wedding day's over. But for all that, I say it would take a pretty strong friendship to make a man risk his life in a half-filled balloon even for the sake of her peace of mind. If I was you, I wouldn't go an inch. I'd stay here until somebody came along and took us off. And after all, it isn't a matter of life and death that the lady's mind should be relieved. Don't go."

"Madam," said I, "you don't understand my feelings on the subject, and it is quite natural that you shouldn't; but I assure you that that lady's peace of mind is of the greatest importance to me, and I shall try to get over to the mainland and let her know there is no reason for her apprehensions, which have probably already seized upon her, and which must grow greater and more distressing hour by hour and day by day."

She looked at me, drew a deep breath, and said no more.

"I can't get hold of the valve-cord," said Crimrose, approaching; "it's broken off too high up; but that won't matter, for I don't believe you'll want to let out any gas; in fact, I think it will be prudent for you to load up with some stones for ballast so as to be sure you won't go too high. Then if you find yourself getting too low, you can throw out some of them."

"Humph!" said Mrs. Pocock; "you think he'll want ballast, do you?"

The radiant Crimrose apparently did not hear this contemptuous remark. "Before you start," said he, "I'll go over there to that tree where I put my writing-desk, and add something to my letter to Jeannette. The first thing I want you to do, Harry, when you reach land, is to put that letter in the nearest post-office. Then you can attend to getting a vessel for us. Jeannette must be thought of before anybody else."

He came back very soon to where Mr. Pocock and I were looking for suitable stones for ballast.

"How are you going to carry this letter, Harry?" said he; "put it in some pocket where you will be sure it will not drop out, or get wet if there should be rain."

Before I could answer, Mrs. Pocock spoke. "It ought to be sewed up in a piece of oiled silk," she said; "for even if it got damp, she might not be able to read it. I've something that will be just the thing. It's an oil-skin bathing-cap which I brought in case there should be too much wind or rain for my bonnet. Give it to me, and I'll sew it up in a jiffy."

"Thank you very much," said Crimrose, and handed her the letter.

Mr. Pocock now assured me that I need feel no anxiety about those I left behind me. The tide was receding, and he had examined the boat and found that the water in her had not risen high enough to wet the floor of the little cabin, so he and his wife could occupy one of the compartments that night, and Mr. Crimrose the other, and they would be just as comfortable as if they had been at home.

In half an hour the grappling-line had been lengthened, the ballast put into the car, and everything made ready for me to start; but the watchmaker's wife had not yet finished sewing up the letter in the oil-skin cap. Her husband called to her, and she came running toward us.

"Here it is," she said; "and you may get soaking wet yourself, but the letter will be all right. I fastened a string to the bag by which you can hang it around your neck, where it will be just as safe as if it was a watch."

"If you want a good watch," said the watchmaker, "I can lend you one, though I don't know really that anything extra in the way of a watch would be of service to you, not taking any interest in the influence of altitudes on balance-wheels."

I declined his offer, and going to the balloon, clambered into it. The rest of the party came up to me, and shook hands with me most cordially, wishing me a safe and quick journey. The watchmaker's wife was the last.

"You take my blessing with you, young man," said she, "and if ever I hope that anything would be of good to anybody, I hope that may be of good to you," and I could see tears in her eyes as she pressed my hand. I felt in my heart that she was a good old woman.

They loosened the rope, and as it slipped under the root of the tree, I began to rise very slowly. I saw that I had too much ballast in the car, and I threw out some of the stones. Then I went up until the rope with the grapnel at the end of it had been let out to its full length.

"Are you ready?" cried Crimrose, from below.

"All right," I answered. He unhooked the grapnel, and I sailed away, free from every earthly tie.

Clouds were spreading over the eastern sky, but it was still clear in the west, and it seemed to me as I looked out in the direction in which the moderate but steady breeze was wafting me, that I was slowly drifting into the sunset, and in my present state of mind that seemed a very good place to drift into. I did not care to give more than one look back at the island, because it grated upon my feelings to see Crimrose standing there wildly waving his handkerchief.

On and on I went, never rising so high above the water that I could not have touched it with my grappling-iron if I had let it down, and steadily moving westward. As it grew darker, I strained my eyes to discover any indications of the coast, but I could see nothing before me but the sky and the sea, still touched with the fading yellow and pink.

I now opened the basket which Mrs. Pocock had put into the car, and found that she had provided for me somewhat at the expense of those I had left behind. It contained our only remaining bottle of wine and the whole of a chicken, besides a jar of marmalade which I thought would be very much missed by Crimrose.

I made a good supper, and determining to follow the example of the watchmaker's wife, I made myself comfortable in the bottom of the car. There was nothing else to do; for the dark night was now fast settling about me, and when I last looked over the side of the car I could scarcely see the glimmer of the water below me.

I hoped that nothing would happen to me, and that I would safely reach land and perform my mission, but I could not prevent the thought coming to me that if I should slowly sink into the sea, or should disappear into the black sky above me, it would be a great relief to a soul, troubled without reason, but still sadly troubled. I did not sleep much; in fact, the night was passed in a succession of broken naps. Sometimes the car swayed disagreeably, and frequently it would seem to suddenly sink beneath me, making me feel as if I were sitting on a chair whose legs were giving way. Once I awoke with a start, and found that I was wet and that water was splashing about me. It took but a second to comprehend that the car was close to the sea, sometimes brushing the tops of the waves. Instantly I threw over all the stones that remained in the car, and as the water splashed up over me, I for the first time shuddered with fear. But now I rose clear of the sea, and though I sat and peered down with eager watchfulness, I did not approach it again for a long time. With the first glimmer of dawn I could see the waves again. They were not very far below me, and turning to see how I could further lighten the balloon, I threw out my basket of provisions. Then I rose again, but it was not long before I began to settle down nearer and nearer to the water.

It was plain that the gas was, in some way or the other, oozing out of the balloon. As the daylight became stronger, I was positive that I could see to the west indications of a line of coast. If I could but keep the balloon in the air for only an hour more, it might carry me to land. The grapnel was a heavy thing; I drew it in, untied it, and dropped it into the sea. This helped a little, but I soon saw that the car needed further lightening, and I threw out the whole coil of grappling-rope. This sent up both the balloon and my heart; and as the breeze was now very much stronger than when I started, I rapidly approached the land. All desire to melt into the sea or the sky had now disappeared, and I watched the approaching shore with feverish anxiety. I was drawing near to what seemed to be the mouth of a river or narrow inlet, but I was also drawing nearer and nearer to the surface of the sea, and there was nothing else to throw out.

It was not long before I hung barely six feet above the water, and then I saw that the balloon must be lightened or I should never reach the land alive. I quickly cut five or six of the cords on opposite sides of the car and tied them together, then, clambering upon the loop thus made, I cut the remaining cords and let the car drop. This resulted in a grand rise into the air, and I did not come down again until I was over the marshy banks of a little river. This was not at all a good place to land, for with the exception of a hummock here and there, there was nothing solid enough for a foothold. As I slowly came down I lowered myself from the loop in which I had been sitting, and suspended myself from it by my hands. Then, as soon as I approached a hummock I put my foot on it, and gave a spring. This sent me up, and the wind carried me forward, and I covered in my first leap of the sort some twenty or thirty feet. Again and again I repeated this action, sometimes failing to strike a hummock or bunch of grass, but even a kick into the water and mud sent me up a little, and after many efforts and some fruitless splashing I passed the marsh and reached solid ground.

Here my first impulse was to let go of the balloon, but on second thoughts I decided not to release it yet. Before me lay a long stretch of sandy dunes which I must cross, and as I stood, my feet lightly pressing the ground, and the balloon steadily pulling at me so that I could not stand still, I determined to make still further use of it. With a run and a vigorous spring I cleared nearly a dozen yards. My arms were tired, but the motion was exhilarating; I bounded like a hare or a kangaroo. In a wonderfully short time I had gone over a mile or two of waste land, and saw before me a house, with a man hurrying out of the door.

As I neared the house I made a bound which carried me easily over a fence, and the man stood looking at me in dumb amazement. My arms now began to feel as if they would be torn from my body, and I shouted to him to come quickly to cut the silk in the balloon. My respect for the Pococks made me anxious to save it, at least what was left of it, if it were possible.

The man comprehended the situation, and as I held back, he ran up and made a long gash in the balloon as high as he could reach, and then he took hold of the rope to help me hold it. In a few minutes the great silken folds were flopping on the ground.

I was nearly exhausted with excitement and fatigue, but the man and his wife gave me a warm breakfast, and I told my tale, frequently interrupted by their exclamations of astonishment. In return, the man, who was a small coast farmer, informed me that he knew the island on which we had been cast, and that if he had anything but a row-boat he would be glad to go out and rescue my companions, but there was no one in the neighborhood who owned a sail-boat large enough for such a trip except Captain Archibald Wharton, who lived about a mile up the coast. He had a big fishing-boat.

Together we went to the fisherman's house. We found Captain Archie, as he was called, but at first he would not believe the tale I told him. However, when my companion asserted that he had seen me arrive with the balloon, the fisherman was obliged to give faith to that much of the story; and as the rest could be no more fabulous, he expressed his willingness to do what he could to bring in my companions. But his boat was not at home; it had been hired to a fisherman down the coast, who would not return with it until that evening, and then, of course, he could not start out at night. He was opposed to working on Sunday; but he said that if his boat got in in time, he would start out the next day and would probably bring my friends to land before nightfall. I had hoped to get a boat to go immediately to the island, but as there was nothing better to be done, I arranged with Captain Archie, paying him a part of his price in advance in order to hold him to his bargain; and then having done all that I could in this line, I inquired for the nearest railroad station. This was five miles away, but my friend, the farmer, agreed to take me over in his wagon, also promising to keep the balloon safely until it was called for.

I did not mail Crimrose's letter to Jeannette; for I reflected as this was Saturday and there would be no mails to-morrow, she would not receive the letter until Monday. So I determined to take it to her myself. This would suit me in every way, for my home, as well as hers, was in Boston.

It was about the middle of the afternoon when I reached the city, and at first I thought I would go home to array myself in attire more suitable to the occasion than the rough yachting-suit smeared with the mud of the marsh. But all this would take time, and I went immediately to deliver my letter to Jeannette; and as I knew she would want to know everything about our mishap, I asked to see her. She came into the room with outstretched hand. If she had been anxious or troubled, it had made her look lovelier.

"What has happened!" she exclaimed, gazing at my untidy figure; "has there been an accident?"

"Yes," I said, "but nobody has been hurt, and I bring you a letter from Mr. Crimrose."

I took from my breast pocket the oil-skin cap of the watchmaker's wife, and removing the string from around my neck I handed the package to Jeannette.

"You can rip it open better than I can," I said.

Jeannette laughed. "What a funny little mail-bag," she said. And before she would even attempt to open it she made me tell her the whole history of our adventure.

I made the narrative as short as I could, touching very lightly upon my homeward balloon trip. Jeannette then opened the bag, saying that when she had read her letter she would want to ask me some questions about myself and the balloon.

I could not sit and look at her read Crimrose's letter. During all the time I had been talking to her there had been growing on my mind the feeling that after all it was a pity that I had been able to lighten the balloon. The next day was Sunday, and Crimrose would probably be in Boston that night. He would see her on Monday and Tuesday, and on Wednesday they would be married. I turned away from Jeannette, took up a book, and gazed steadfastly at its pages.

"Two!" she said presently, in a tone of some surprise, and then for a minute I heard nothing but the rustling of paper. Then there was another little exclamation, and I heard the cutting of a second envelope. In a few minutes I heard Jeannette suddenly push back her chair. I looked and saw her standing, her face flushed, and an open letter in her hand. Then, without looking at me, she quickly turned toward the door and went out of the room.

If Crimrose, instead of adding to the letter he had already prepared, had sent another (which was natural enough, for he must have had a good deal to say), what could he have put into his second epistle which would have caused Jeannette to treat me with such abrupt discourtesy?

She may not have comprehended the fact that I had risked my life to bring her those letters, but she must have understood that my service was not a common one, and nothing her lover could have said to her should have made her forget that at least I merited ordinary civility.

I waited some time and then I rang the bell and sent to ask if Miss Collins had any further commands for me. The servant soon returned with the message that her mistress asked to be excused from coming down. Feeling very much like a dog who had been kicked out of doors, I went home.

I was angry and hurt, and came to the very sensible determination to travel and separate myself as much as possible from the causes of my pain and humiliation. But I did not start on the next day as I had intended, nor did I go on the day following; a good reason for my delay was my desire to hear something about the party I had left on the island. I could not go from Boston without knowing whether or not they had been safely brought to the mainland. I expected that Crimrose would write or telegraph to me as soon as he found it possible, but I heard nothing until I saw, in an afternoon paper on Monday, a short account of the adventure, which stated that Captain Wharton had brought away the desert islanders on Sunday evening. I was quite sure that Crimrose wrote this account, because it was in his style, and contained but a slight reference to my balloon trip, about which he, of course, knew but little.

·The next morning Crimrose came to see me, and explained his not writing by saying that he had been very much pressed for time and knew that I would see the account in the paper. He did not seem to be pressed for time now, for he made himself comfortable in a large chair and lighted a cigar. This surprised me, for he was nearly always in a hurry, and I asked him if he had already finished the business which had made it so important for him to get back to Boston.

"Oh!" said he, "you mean preparing to be married. The wedding is postponed."

"Postponed!" I exclaimed.

"Yes," said he; "it was simply impossible for me to get ready in the little time I had. You haven't any idea what I have to do. I can do as much in a short time as any man can, but it is ridiculous to attempt the impossible."

"And Miss Collins!" I cried; "what does she think of this?"

"Oh, she does not mind it," said Crimrose; "I don't believe she's ready: women never are. Anyway, she agrees to the postponement."

"For how long?" I asked.

"For about a week, perhaps, but it isn't quite settled yet. The fact is, Miss Collins is a good deal upset by the dangers to which I have been exposed, and she does not seem to be able to get her mind down to business. Moreover, —and I don't mind saying this to you, as you are an old friend, —she seems to be beset with a desire to ask questions. Never in my life have I passed through such an inquisition. I hate answering questions and always did. There was not an incident of that wretched adventure that she did not want to know, and afterward to find out its causes and effects and everything about it. I suppose this is not to be wondered at, for she is naturally nervous, and it is a very good thing that we agreed to postpone the wedding. She is not in a state of mind for it now. Twelve o'clock! I had no idea it was so late, and I have an engagement at half-past."

As there was to be no wedding on the next day, I did not leave Boston. I spent several days in a very unpleasant state of mind. There constantly arose within me a desire to kill Crimrose; but as there was really nothing to justify the attempt, I endeavored to smother this desire. It was plain that my friend had no suspicion of my feelings toward him, for on Saturday he called on me, valise in hand.

"Where are you going?" I said, pushing back from my breakfast-table.

"I take the eleven o'clock train for Quebec," he

said; "I want some bracing air, and can't wait for it here. I need a change, anyway."

"Quebec!" I exclaimed; "but you can't get back by Wednesday."

"Of course not," said he. "Oh, I see. That's postponed again."

"Postponed again!" I cried, rising to my feet.

"Oh yes," he answered. "The fact is neither of us is ready for it. The engagement is — well — I may say prolonged or perhaps — well, as you will probably get varying accounts, I will state plainly that the engagement is set aside for the present. Miss Collins is — well, she has not treated me well. She has put interrogations and made statements that a man of spirit cannot submit to. Of course I do not wish to say anything against her, but I cannot marry anybody in the frame of mind in which Miss Collins is at present. All this of course is —"

"Crimrose!" I cried, advancing toward him, "are you playing false to Miss Collins? Are you daring to trifle —"

"Stop! Stop!" said he; "don't work yourself into a passion. It isn't any affair of yours, anyway, but I don't mind telling you, since you are getting so excited about it, that I hadn't anything to do with laying this affair on the table. She put the motion, and as she has ever so many more voices than I have, it was carried. But it is satisfactory all around, and when we reopen the matter we will begin afresh. Good by; I will see you before long."

I did not answer, for my head was in a whirl. Some time during the morning I went to take a walk, but I know I did not finish my breakfast. For days I was as a ship which, without compass or rudder or sails, drifts in a calm. I did not know what I did or why I did it instead of doing something else.

At last I had a visit, and this was well; for if no one had come to see me, I would have seen nobody. My visitor was the watchmaker's wife, and at first I did not recognize her, nor after we had shaken hands did I remember her name until she mentioned it.

"I have been trying for a good while," she said, "to find your address so that Mr. Pocock or me could come to see you or write to you. We want to pay you our share of the money you gave Captain Wharton in advance for going after us."

At this it struck me that Crimrose had not offered to pay his portion of said money.

"And more than that," the old lady continued, "we want to tell you how greatly obliged we are to you for doing what you did and sending a boat for us, and how thankful we are that you got over safe and sound. I could not sleep that night for thinking of you hanging under that half-empty balloon. But I don't believe I would have found where you lived if it had not been for Miss Collins. I knew her address, for I saw it on Mr. Crimrose's letter and remembered it."

"And you have seen her!" I exclaimed.

"Oh yes, yes," said the old lady, looking down in her lap as she smoothed one mittened hand with the fingers of the other; "I have seen her and had a long talk with her, and have heard all about the breaking off of the engagement."

"Breaking off!" I exclaimed; "is it entirely broken off?"

"Oh yes, yes," answered Mrs. Pocock; "and I am sure it is a great blessing for which everybody ought to be thankful. If she had married that Crimrose man, my very heart would have bled for her. I did not know him long, but I saw enough of him to understand him through and through. It did not need anything more than to hear what he said when he found out that I had given you that cold chicken and the jar of marmalade. Goodness! I could have thrown a tea-kettle at him. But it's all right now, it's all right now."

"But Miss Collins," I asked; "what does she think of it?"

"That's hard to say," answered the old lady; "that's pretty hard to say; but of course she's glad the match is broken off, because now she knows Crimrose as well as I do; but it's natural enough that she should be a good deal upset; anybody would be in a case like that, and I think it is the duty of her friends to go and cheer her up. You, sir, for instance, if you was to go and see her and talk to her cheerfully and tell her all about your balloon trip, — that I know she wants to hear about, none of us having been able to tell her anything of it except the starting, — it would do her a lot of good."

"I go to see her!" I exclaimed; "do you know, madam — " and then I hesitated. But though a comparative stranger, the old lady was so sympathetic and so kind, that I went on, "Do you know that she treated me rudely when I was there last, and declined to see me when I left?"

"Oh don't mind that," said Mrs. Pocock; "don't mind that. She told me all about that. You ought not to take any notice of it at all. The letters you brought her upset her to a degree that it made her lose control of herself. You see I — I mean it wasn't expected that she should read her letters when you or anybody was by. You mustn't think of that at all. I know all about it. It wasn't any feeling against you that made her act that way. Go to see her, and you will find out that it wasn't. She will treat you just as polite as ever she did, and it's your duty to go, sir; for I know she looks upon you as one of her best friends, for she told me so herself."

When Mrs. Pocock left me she urged me, if ever I happened to be near Barnville, to step in and see her and Mr. Pocock: they would be so glad to see me, and the village was not half an hour from Boston.

It was an early hour for a call when, the next morning, I presented myself at Miss Collins's door; but I was admitted, and turning over in my mind everything that I thought would amuse and interest her in the story of my adventure without agitating her nerves or causing her to think that I was trying to make a hero of myself, I awaited her coming.

Jeannette was not at her ease with me, but this was not to be wondered at, considering how intimate I had been with her and with Crimrose; but as the watchmaker's wife had told me, she had no unfriendly feelings toward me, and, in fact, apologized for having left me so abruptly when I had called before. It was a sudden nervous attack, she said, and I could readily understand that if Crimrose had behaved as badly as he must have done to justify her breaking off the engagement, he had probably put something into his letters which had shocked the poor girl. It might be that I would yet kill Crimrose, for a more beautiful woman than Jeannette never lived, nor one more worthy to have villains slain in her behalf.

After a little while Jeannette's stiffness wore off, and I told her everything about my balloon trip. She was so interested and so beautiful that I did not even omit the washing of the waves in the darkness, against the bottom of the car, and my dreadful fears in the morning, that even in sight of the land, the balloon would be too weak to hold me up, and I should sink helpless into the sea. There was moisture in her eyes, her lips were parted, and she leaned forward to look at me.

"Oh! how could you dare all that?" she said; "you must have known the dangers. How did you have the courage to float out in that way into the dreadful mysteries of the night and the sea?"

I could not help the answer that came to my lips.

"I did it for you," I said.

Slipping thus from the brink of the precipice, down I went.

"It is dreadful," said Jeannette, five minutes afterward, with tears in her eyes, but half laughing; "you shouldn't have spoken so soon. It seems like —"

"Never mind," said I, checking her; "it could not be helped, and I wish I had spoken a year ago."

"I wish you had," whispered Jeannette.

It was at least half an hour after this, that among all the wonders of this new heavenly world which I had just entered, nothing surprised me more than that she should have been so little surprised when I had opened my heart to her.

"How could I be," said she, "after the letter you brought me?"

"Letter!" I cried; "did Crimrose —"

"Crimrose!" she said; "what utter nonsense! But I see that you know nothing. I will get you the letter which gave me the nervous shock."

She brought it; it ran thus: —

Miss Jeannette Collins: —

My dear young lady: I am a married woman whose husband, Sylvester Pocock, does business in Barnville, and is known all over that country, and I have been cast away on an island in a way that I haven't time to tell you about, but of which you will soon hear all the particulars. I am in a great hurry, having to write secretly and unobserved, and without stopping to mince matters I beg and implore you with all the earnestness, which one woman who knows what true love is, can appeal with to one who I believe doesn't, not having had a fair chance, not to marry Mr. Crimrose, not, at least, until you have a chance to think over things after what I tell you. That feather-bed of a Crimrose is not the man who really loves you. I have so little time that I have to speak strong; he is a selfish brute and loves nobody but himself. Take time to try him, my dear young lady, and you will find that out for yourself. Mr. Elliot, the gentleman who will bring you this, if you ever get it, is the man who truly loves you. I have so little time that I am obliged to put things strong. He doesn't know it, but I have found out that he loves you from the bottom of his heart, that he would cast himself into the middle of the sea to save you from one sleepless night, and so far as anybody can tell, he may do it. He is going to risk his life to keep you from being worried and anxious.

He is the modestest man and the best friend that I have ever met in all my life, and I say boldly, without caring what happens or what people think of me, that if you marry Crimrose instead of Elliot, you will make a mistake that will bring you years of misery. I can't make this strong enough, for I haven't time and don't know how; but, my dear young lady, I beg and implore you, stop long enough to give your true lover a chance. I have given you warning, look into the matter yourself. Mr. Elliot has loved you for ever so long, and Crimrose never can do it; it isn't in him.

Nobody knows I am writing this, and it may be drowned in the sea with the noble young man who risks his life to take it to you. It is all mixed up, and you may think it's strong, but it comes from the heart of a woman who doesn't want to see any other woman, even a total stranger, make the mistake that you are on the brink of.

Yours in haste,

Sarah Pocock.

I stood aghast. "And this," I exclaimed, "was the second letter!"

"Of course," said Jeannette.

"And you — knew — "

"I expected, — I could not be certain," said Jeannette demurely. "I had suspected something of the sort long ago, and in a manner had expected — but nothing ever happened."

"Bless that watchmaker's wife!" said I.

On the first day that I could get an hour or two to spare, I went to Barnville, and, without any trouble, found Mr. Pocock's shop. Pocock is a good man, and he had sense enough to stay in the shop while I sat in the little back parlor and talked to his wife. It was a long interview, and very warm on both sides, but she was such an elderly person no one could object to that.

"Well," said she, as I was leaving, and she stood holding me by the hand, "it gladdens my heart to think that there is to be another true, loving couple in this world. And I am sure I ought to feel so, for it is very seldom that a woman has had the chance that I have had of making two men happy."

"Two men?" I asked.

"Yes," said she; "you and Mr. Pocock."

ASAPH

ABOUT a hundred feet back from the main street of a village in New Jersey there stood a very good white house. Halfway between it and the sidewalk was a large chestnut tree, which had been the pride of Mr. Himes, who built the house, and was now the pride of Mrs. Himes, his widow, who lived there.

Under the tree was a bench and on the bench were two elderly men, both smoking pipes, and each one of them leaning forward with his elbows on his knees. One of these, Thomas Rooper by name, was a small man with gray side whiskers, a rather thin face, and very good clothes. His pipe was a meerschaum, handsomely colored, with a long amber tip. He had bought that pipe while on a visit to Philadelphia during the great Centennial Exposition; and if any one noticed it and happened to remark what a fine pipe it was, that person would be likely to receive a detailed account of the circumstances of its purchase, with an appendix relating to the Main building, the Art building, the Agricultural building, and many other salient points of the great Exposition which commemorated the centennial of our national independence.

The other man, Asaph Scantle, was of a different type. He was a little older than his companion, but if his hair were gray it did not show very much, as his rather long locks were of a sandy hue and his full face was clean shaven, at least on Wednesdays and Sundays. He was tall, round-shouldered, and his clothes were not good, possessing very evident claims to a position on the retired list. His pipe consisted of a common clay bowl with a long reed stem.

For some minutes the two men continued to puff together as if they were playing a duet upon tobacco pipes, and then Asaph, removing his reed from his lips, remarked, "What you ought to do, Thomas, is to marry money."

"There's sense in that," replied the other; "but you wasn't the first to think of it."

Asaph, who knew very well that Mr. Rooper never allowed any one to suppose that he received suggestions from without, took no notice of the last remark, but went on: "Lookin' at the matter in a friendly way, it seems to me it stands to reason that when the shingles on a man's house is so rotten that the rain comes through into every room on the top floor, and when the plaster on the ceilin' is tumblin' down more or less all the time and the window sashes is all loose, and things generally in a condition that he can't let that house without spendin' at least a year's rent on it to git it into decent order, and when a man's got to the time of life —"

"There's nothin' the matter with the time of life," said Thomas; "that's all right."

"What I was goin' to say was," continued Asaph,

"that when a man gits to the time of life when he knows what it is to be comfortable in his mind as well as his body, and that time comes to sensible people as soon as they git fairly growed up, he don't want to give up his good room in the tavern and all the privileges of the house, and go to live on his own property and have the plaster come down on his own head and the rain come down on the coverlet of his own bed."

"No, he don't," said Thomas; "and what is more, he isn't goin' to do it. But what I git from the rent of that house is what I have to live on; there's no gittin' around that pint."

"Well, then," said Asaph, "if you don't marry money, what are you goin' to do? You can't go back to your old business."

"I never had but one business," said Thomas. "I lived with my folks until I was a good deal more than growed up; and when the war broke out I went as sutler to the rigiment from this place; and all the money I made I put into my property in the village here. That's what I've lived on ever since. There's no more war, so there's no more sutlers, except away out West where I wouldn't go; and there are no more folks, for they are all dead; and if what Mrs. McJimsey says is true, there'll be no more tenants in my house after the first of next November. For when the McJimseys go on account of want of general repairs, it is not to be expected that anybody else will come there. There's nobody in this place that can stand as much as the McJimseys can."

"Consequently," said Asaph, deliberately filling his

pipe, "it stands to reason that there ain't nothin' for you to do but marry money."

Thomas Rooper took his pipe from his mouth and sat up straight. Gazing steadfastly at his companion, he remarked, "If you think that is such a good thing to do, why don't you do it yourself? There can't be anybody much harder up than you are."

"The law's agin' my doin' it," said Asaph. "A man can't marry his sister."

"Are you thinkin' of Marietta Himes?" asked Mr. Rooper.

"That's the one I'm thinkin' of," said Asaph. "If you can think of anybody better, I'd like you to mention her."

Mr. Rooper did not immediately speak. He presently asked: "What do you call money?"

"Well," said Asaph, with a little hesitation, "considerin' the circumstances, I should say that in a case like this about fifteen hundred a year, a first-rate house, with not a loose shingle on it nor a crack anywhere, a good garden and an orchard, two cows, a piece of meadow land on the other side of the creek, and all the clothes a woman need have, is money."

Thomas shrugged his shoulders. "Clothes!" he said. "If she marries she'll go out of black, and then she'll have to have new ones, and lots of 'em. That would make a big hole in her money, Asaph."

The other smiled. "I always knowed you was a far-seein' feller, Thomas; but it stands to reason that Marietta's got a lot of clothes that was on hand before she went into mournin', and she's not the kind of woman to waste 'em. She'll be twistin' 'em about and makin' 'em over to suit the fashions, and it won't be like her to be buyin' new colored goods when she's got plenty of 'em already."

There was now another pause in the conversation and then Mr. Rooper remarked: "Mrs. Himes must be gettin' on pretty well in years."

"She's not a young woman," said Asaph; "but if she was much younger she wouldn't have you, and if she was much older you wouldn't have her. So it strikes me she's just about the right pint."

"How old was John Himes when he died?" asked Thomas.

"I don't exactly know that; but he was a lot older than Marietta."

Thomas shook his head. "It strikes me," said he, "that John Himes had a hearty constitution and hadn't ought to died as soon as he did. He fell away a good deal in the last years of his life."

"And considerin' that he died of consumption, he had a right to fall away," said Asaph. "If what you are drivin' at, Thomas, is that Marietta isn't a good housekeeper and hasn't the right sort of notions of feedin', look at me. I've lived with Marietta just about a year, and in that time I have gained forty-two pounds. Now, of course, I ain't unreasonable, and don't mean to say that you would gain forty-two pounds in a year, 'cause you ain't got the frame and bone to put it on; but it wouldn't surprise me a bit if you was to gain twenty, or even twenty-five pounds in eighteen months, anyway; and more than that you ought not to ask, Thomas, considerin' your height and general build."

"Isn't Marietta Himes a good deal of a free-thinker?" asked Thomas.

"A what?" cried Asaph. "You mean an infidel?"

"No," said Thomas, "I don't charge nobody with nothin' more than there's reason for; but they do say that she goes sometimes to one church and sometimes to another, and that if there was a Catholic church in this village she would go to that. And who's goin' to say where a woman will turn up when she don't know her own mind better than that?"

Asaph colored a little. "The place where Marietta will turn up," said he warmly, "is on a front seat in the kingdom of heaven; and if the people that talk about her will mend their ways, they'll see that I am right. You need not trouble yourself about that, Thomas. Marietta Himes is pious to the heel."

Mr. Rooper now shifted himself a little on the bench and crossed one leg over the other. "Now look here, Asaph," he said, with a little more animation than he had yet shown, "supposin' all you say is true, have you got any reason to think that Mrs. Himes ain't satisfied with things as they are?"

"Yes, I have," said Asaph. "And I don't mind tellin' you that the thing she's least satisfied with is me. She wants a man in the house; that is nateral. She wouldn't be Marietta Himes if she didn't. When I come to live with her I thought the whole business was settled; but it isn't. I don't suit her. I don't say she's lookin' for another man, but if another man was to come along, and if he was the right kind of a man, it's my opinion she's ready for him. I wouldn't say this to everybody, but I say it to you, Thomas Rooper, 'cause I know what kind of a man you are."

Mr. Rooper did not return the compliment. "I don't wonder your sister ain't satisfied with you," he said, "for you go ahead of all the lazy men I ever saw yet. They was sayin' down at the tavern yesterday, only yesterday, that you could do less work in more time than anybody they ever saw before."

"There's two ways of workin'," said Asaph. "Some people work with their hands and some with their heads."

Thomas grimly smiled. "It strikes me," said he, "that the most headwork you do is with your jaws."

Asaph was not the man to take offence readily, especially when he considered it against his interest to do so, and he showed no resentment at this remark. "'Taint so much my not makin' myself more generally useful," he said, "that Marietta objects to; though, of course, it could not be expected that a man that hasn't got any interest in property would keep workin' at it like a man that has got an interest in it, such as Marietta's husband would have; but it's my general appearance that she don't like. She's told me more than once she didn't so much mind my bein' lazy as lookin' lazy."

"I don't wonder she thinks that way," said Thomas. "But look here, Asaph, do you suppose that if Marietta Himes was to marry a man, he would really come into her property?"

"There ain't nobody that knows my sister better than I know her, and I can say, without any fear of bein' contradicted, that when she gives herself to a man the good-will and fixtures will be included."

Thomas Rooper now leaned forward with his elbows on his knees without smoking, and Asaph Scantle leaned forward with his elbows on his knees without smoking. And thus they remained, saying nothing to each other, for the space of some ten minutes.

Asaph was a man who truly used his head a great deal more than he used his hands. He had always been a shiftless fellow, but he was no fool, and this his sister found out soon after she asked him to come and make his home with her. She had not done this because she wanted a man in the house, for she had lived two or three years without that convenience and had not felt the need of it. But she heard that Asaph was in very uncomfortable circumstances, and she had sent for him solely for his own good. The arrangement proved to be a very good one for her brother, but not a good one for her. She had always known that Asaph's head was his main dependence, but she was just beginning to discover that he liked to use his head so that other people's hands should work for him.

"There ain't nobody comin' to see your sister, is there?" asked Thomas suddenly.

"Not a livin' soul," said Asaph, "except women, married folk, and children. But it has always surprised me that nobody did come; but just at this minute the field's clear and the gate's open."

"Well," said Mr. Rooper, "I'll think about it."

"That's right," said Asaph, rubbing his knees with his hands. "That's right. But now tell me, Thomas

Rooper, supposin' you get Marietta, what are you goin' to do for me?"

"For you?" exclaimed the other. "What have you got to do with it?"

"A good deal," said Asaph. "If you get Marietta with her fifteen hundred a year, and it wouldn't surprise me if it was eighteen hundred, and her house and her garden and her cattle and her field and her furniture, with not a leg loose nor a scratch, you will get her because I proposed her to you, and because I backed you up afterward. And now then, I want to know what you are goin' to do for me?"

"What do you want?" asked Thomas.

"The first thing I want," said Asaph, "is a suit of clothes. These clothes is disgraceful."

"You are right there," said Mr. Rooper. "I wonder your sister lets you come around in front of the house. But what do you mean by clothes; winter clothes or summer clothes?"

"Winter," said Asaph, without hesitation. "I don't count summer clothes. And when I say a suit of clothes, I mean shoes and hat and underclothes."

Mr. Rooper gave a sniff. "I wonder you don't say overcoat," he remarked.

"I do say overcoat," replied Asaph. "A suit of winter clothes is a suit of clothes that you can go out into the weather in without missin' nothin'."

Mr. Rooper smiled sarcastically. "Is there anything else you want?" he asked.

"Yes," said Asaph, decidedly; "there is. I want a umbrella."

"Cotton or silk?"

Asaph hesitated. He had never had a silk umbrella in his hand in his life. He was afraid to strike too high, and he answered, "I want a good stout gingham."

Mr. Rooper nodded his head. "Very good," he said. "And is that all?"

"No," said Asaph, "it ain't all. There is one more thing I want, and that is a dictionary."

The other man rose to his feet. "Upon my word," he exclaimed, "I never before saw a man that would sell his sister for a dictionary. And what you want with a dictionary is past my conceivin'."

"Well, it ain't past mine," said Asaph. "For more than ten years I have wanted a dictionary. If I had a dictionary I could make use of my head in a way that I can't now. There is books in this house, but amongst 'em there is no dictionary. If there had been one, I'd been a different man by this time from what I am now, and like as not Marietta wouldn't have wanted any other man in the house but me."

Mr. Rooper stood looking upon the ground; and Asaph, who had also arisen, waited for him to speak. "You are a graspin' man, Asaph," said Thomas. "But there is another thing I'd like to know: if I give you them clothes, you don't want them before she's married?"

"Yes, I do," said Asaph. "If I come to the weddin', I can't wear these things. I have got to have them first."

Mr. Rooper gave his head a little twist. "There's many a slip 'twixt the cup and the lip," said he.

"Yes," said Asaph; "and there's different cups and

different lips. But what's more, if I was to be best man, which would be nateral, considerin' I'm your friend and her brother, you wouldn't want me standin' up in this rig. And that's puttin' it in your own point of view, Thomas."

"It strikes me," said the other, "that I could get a best man that would furnish his own clothes; but we will see about that. There's another thing, Asaph," he said abruptly; "what are Mrs. Himes's views concernin' pipes?"

This question startled and frightened Asaph. He knew that his sister could not abide the smell of tobacco and that Mr. Rooper was an inveterate smoker.

"That depends," said he, "on the kind of tobacco. I don't mind sayin' that Marietta isn't partial to the kind of tobacco I smoke. But I ain't a moneyed man and I can't afford to buy nothin' but cheap stuff. But when it comes to a meerschaum pipe and the very finest Virginia or North Carolina smoking tobacco, such as a moneyed man would be likely to use —"

At this moment there came from the house the sound of a woman's voice, not loud, but clear and distinct, and it said "Asaph."

This word sent through Mr. Rooper a gentle thrill such as he did not remember ever having felt before. There seemed to be in it a suggestion, a sort of prophecy, of what appeared to him as an undefined and chaotic bliss. He was not a fanciful man, but he could not help imagining himself standing alone under that chestnut tree and that voice calling "Thomas."

Upon Asaph the effect was different. The interruption was an agreeable one in one way, because it cut short his attempted explanation of the tobacco question; but in another way he knew that it meant the swinging of an axe, and that was not pleasant.

Mr. Rooper walked back to the tavern in a cogitative state of mind. "That Asaph Scantle," he said to himself, "has got a headpiece, there's no denying it. If it had not been for him I do not believe I should have thought of his sister; at least not until the McJimseys had left my house, and then it might have been too late."

Marietta Himes was a woman with a gentle voice and an appearance and demeanor indicative of a general softness of disposition, but beneath this mild exterior there was a great deal of firmness of purpose. Asaph had not seen very much of his sister since she had grown up and married; and when he came to live with her he thought that he was going to have things pretty much his own way. But it was not long before he entirely changed his mind.

Mrs. Himes was of moderate height, pleasant countenance, and a figure inclined to plumpness. Her dark hair, in which there was not a line of gray, was brushed down smoothly on each side of her face, and her dress, while plain, was extremely neat. In fact, everything in the house and on the place was extremely neat, except Asaph.

She was in the bright little dining-room which looked out on the flower garden, preparing the table for supper, placing every plate, dish, glass, and cup with as much care and exactness as if a civil engineer had drawn a plan on the tablecloth with places marked for the position of each article.

As she finished her work by placing a chair on each side of the table, a quiet smile, the result of a train of thought in which she had been indulging for the past half-hour, stole over her face. She passed through the kitchen, with a glance at the stove to see if the tea-kettle had begun to boil, and going out of the back door, she walked over to the shed where her brother was splitting kindling wood.

"Asaph," said Mrs. Himes, "if I were to give you a good suit of clothes, would you promise me that you would never smoke when wearing them?"

Her brother looked at her in amazement. "Clothes!" he repeated.

"Mr. Himes was about your size," said his sister, "and he left a good many clothes, which are most of them very good and carefully packed away, so that I am sure there is not a moth hole in any one of them. I have several times thought, Asaph, that I might give you some of his clothes; but it did seem to me a desecration to have the clothes of such a man, who was so particular and nice, filled and saturated with horrible tobacco smoke which he detested. But now you are getting to be so awful shabby, I do not see how I can stand it any longer. But one thing I will not do, I will not have Mr. Himes's clothes smelling of tobacco as yours do, and not only your own tobacco, but Mr. Rooper's."

"I think," said Asaph, "that you are not exactly right just there. What you smell about me is my smoke. Thomas Rooper never uses anything but the finest scented and delicatest brands. I think that if you come to get used to his tobacco smoke you would like it. But as to my takin' off my clothes and puttin' on a different suit every time I want to light my pipe, that's pretty hard lines, it seems to me."

"It would be a good deal easier to give up the pipe," said his sister.

"I will do that," said Asaph, "when you give up tea. But you know as well as I do that there's no use of either of us a-tryin' to change our comfortable habits at our time of life."

"I kept on hoping," said Mrs. Himes, "that you would feel yourself that you were not fit to be seen by decent people, and that you would go to work and earn at least enough money to buy yourself some clothes. But as you don't seem inclined to do that, I thought I would make you this offer. But you must understand that I will not have you smoke in Mr. Himes's clothes."

Asaph stood thinking, the head of his axe resting upon the ground, a position which suited him. He was in a little perplexity. Marietta's proposition seemed to interfere somewhat with the one he had made to Thomas Rooper. Here was a state of affairs which required most careful consideration. "I've been arrangin' about some clothes," he said presently; "for I know very well I need 'em; but I don't know just yet how it will turn out."

"I hope, Asaph," said Marietta quickly, "that you are not thinking of going into debt for clothing, and I know that you haven't been working to earn money. What arrangements have you been making?"

"That's my private affair," said Asaph, "but there's no debt in it. It is all fair and square—

cash down, so to speak; though, of course; it's not cash, but work. But, as I said before, that isn't settled."

"I am afraid, Asaph," said his sister, "that if you have to do the work first you will never get the clothes, and so you might as well come back to my offer."

Asaph came back to it and thought about it very earnestly. If by any chance he could get two suits of clothes, he would then feel that he had a head worth having. "What would you say," he said presently, "if when I wanted to smoke I was to put on a long duster — I guess Mr. Himes had dusters — and a nightcap and rubbers? I'd agree to hang the duster and the cap in the shed here and never smoke without putting 'em on." There was a deep purpose in this proposition, for, enveloped in the long duster, he might sit with Thomas Rooper under the chestnut tree and smoke and talk and plan as long as he pleased, and his companion would not know that he did not need a new suit of clothes.

"Nonsense," said Mrs. Himes; "you must make up your mind to act perfectly fairly, Asaph, or else say you will not accept my offer. But if you don't accept it, I can't see how you can keep on living with me."

"What do you mean by clothes, Marietta?" he asked.

"Well, I mean a complete suit, of course," said she.

"Winter or summer?"

"I hadn't thought of that," Mrs. Himes replied; "but that can be as you choose."

"Overcoat?" asked Asaph.

"Yes," said she, "and cane and umbrella, if you like, and pocket-handkerchiefs too. I will fit you out completely and shall be glad to have you looking like a decent man."

At the mention of the umbrella another line of perplexity showed itself upon Asaph's brow. The idea came to him that if she would add a dictionary he would strike a bargain. Thomas Rooper was certainly a very undecided and uncertain sort of man. But then there came up the thought of his pipe, and he was all at sea again. Giving up smoking was almost the same as giving up eating. "Marietta," said he, "I will think about this."

"Very well," she answered, "but it's my opinion, Asaph, that you ought not to take more than one minute to think about it. However, I will give you until to-morrow morning, and then if you decide that you don't care to look like a respectable citizen, I must have some further talk with you about our future arrangements."

"Make it to-morrow night," said Asaph. And his sister consented.

The next day Asaph was unusually brisk and active; and very soon after breakfast he walked over to the village tavern to see Mr. Rooper.

"Hello!" exclaimed that individual, surprised at his visitor's early appearance at the business centre of the village. "What's started you out? Have you come after them clothes?"

A happy thought struck Asaph. He had made this visit with the intention of feeling his way towards some decision on the important subject of his sister's proposition, and here a way seemed to be opened to him. "Thomas," said he, taking his friend aside, "I am in an awful fix. Marietta can't stand my clothes any longer. If she can't stand them she can't stand me, and when it comes to that, you can see for yourself that I can't help you."

A shade settled upon Mr. Rooper's face. During the past evening he had been thinking and puffing and puffing and thinking until everybody else in the tavern had gone to bed, and he had finally made up his mind that, if he could do it, he would marry Marietta Himes. He had never been very intimate with her or her husband, but he had been to meals in the house, and he remembered the fragrant coffee and the light, puffy, well-baked rolls made by Marietta's own hands; and he thought of the many differences between living in that very good house with that gentle, pleasant-voiced lady and his present life in the village tavern.

And so, having determined that without delay he would, with the advice and assistance of Asaph, begin his courtship, it was natural that he should feel a shock of discouragement when he heard Asaph's announcement that his sister could not endure him in the house any longer. To attack that house and its owner without the friendly offices upon which he depended was an undertaking for which he was not at all prepared.

"I don't wonder at her," he said sharply, "not a bit. But this puts a mighty different face on the thing what we talked about yesterday."

"It needn't," said Asaph quietly. "The clothes

you was goin' to give me wouldn't cost a cent more to-day than they would in a couple of months, say; and when I've got 'em on Marietta will be glad to have me around. Everything can go on just as we bargained for."

Thomas shook his head. "That would be a mighty resky piece of business," he said. "You would be all right, but that's not sayin' that I would; for it strikes me that your sister is about as much a bird in the bush as any flyin' critter."

Asaph smiled. "If the bush was in the middle of a field," said he, "and there was only one boy after the bird, it would be a pretty tough job. But if the bush is in the corner of two high walls, and there's two boys, and one of 'em's got a fishnet what he can throw clean over the bush, why, then the chances is a good deal better. But droppin' figgers, Thomas, and speakin' plain and straightforward, as I always do—"

"About things you want to git," interrupted Thomas.

"About everything," resumed Asaph. "I'll just tell you this: if I don't git decent clothes now to-day, or perhaps to-morrow, I have got to travel out of Marietta's house. I can do it and she knows it. I can go back to Drummondville and git my board for keepin' books in the store and nobody there cares what sort of clothes I wear. But when that happens, your chance of gittin' Marietta goes up higher than a kite."

To the mind of Mr. Rooper this was most conclusive reasoning; but he would not admit it and he did not like it. "Why don't your sister give you clothes?" he said. "Old Himes must have left some."

A thin chill like a needleful of frozen thread ran down Asaph's back. "Mr. Himes's clothes!" he exclaimed. "What in the world are you talkin' about, Thomas Rooper? 'Tain't likely he had many 'cept what he was buried in, and what's left, if there is any, Marietta would no more think of givin' away than she would of hangin' up his funeral wreath for the canary bird to perch on. There's a room up in the garret where she keeps his special things, for she's awful particular, and if there is any of his clothes up there I expect she's got 'em framed."

"If she thinks as much of him as that," muttered Mr. Rooper.

"Now don't git any sech ideas as them into your head, Thomas," said Asaph quickly. "Marietta ain't a woman to rake up the past, and you never need be afraid of her rakin' up Mr. Himes. All of the premises will be hern and yourn except that room in the garret, and it ain't likely she'll ever ask you to go in there."

"The Lord knows I don't want to!" ejaculated Mr. Rooper.

The two men walked slowly to the end of a line of well-used, or, rather, badly used, wooden armchairs which stood upon the tavern piazza, and seated themselves. Mr. Rooper's mind was in a highly perturbed condition. If he accepted Asaph's present proposition he would have to make a considerable outlay with a very shadowy prospect of return.

"If you haven't got the ready money for the clothes," said Asaph, after having given his companion some minutes for silent consideration, "there ain't a man in this village what they would trust sooner at the store for clothes," and then after a pause he added, "or books, which, of course, they can order from town."

At this Mr. Rooper simply shrugged his shoulders. The question of ready money or credit did not trouble him.

At this moment a man in a low phaeton, drawn by a stout gray horse, passed the tavern.

"Who's that?" asked Asaph, who knew everybody in the village.

"That's Doctor Wicker," said Thomas. "He lives over at Timberley. He 'tended John Himes in his last sickness."

"He don't practise here, does he?" said Asaph. "I never see him."

"No; but he was called in to consult." And then the speaker dropped again into cogitation.

After a few minutes Asaph rose. He knew that Thomas Rooper had a slow-working mind and thought it would be well to leave him to himself for awhile. "I'll go home," said he, "and 'tend to my chores, and by the time you feel like comin' up and takin' a smoke with me under the chestnut tree, I reckon you will have made up your mind, and we'll settle this thing. Fer if I have got to go back to Drummondville, I s'pose I'll have to pack up this afternoon."

"If you'd say pack off instead of pack up," remarked the other, "you'd come nearer the facts, considerin' the amount of your personal property. But I'll be up there in an hour or two."

When Asaph came within sight of his sister's house, he was amazed to see a phaeton and a gray horse standing in front of the gate. From this it was easy to infer that the doctor was in the house. What on earth could have happened? Was anything the matter with Marietta? And if so, why did she send for a physician who lived at a distance, instead of Doctor McIlvaine, the village doctor? In a very anxious state of mind Asaph reached the gate, and irresolutely went into the yard. His impulse was to go to the house and see what had happened; but he hesitated. He felt that Marietta might object to having a comparative stranger know that such an exceedingly shabby fellow was her brother. And, besides, his sister could not have been overtaken by any sudden illness. She had always appeared perfectly well, and there would have been no time during his brief absence from the house to send over to Timberley for a doctor.

So he sat down under the chestnut tree to consider this strange condition of affairs. "Whatever it is," he said to himself, "it's nothin' suddint, and it's bound to be chronic, and that'll skeer Thomas. I wish I hadn't asked him to come up here. The best thing for me to do will be to pretend that I have been sent to git somethin' at the store, and go straight back and keep him from comin' up."

But Asaph was a good deal quicker to think than to move, and he still sat with brows wrinkled and mind beset by doubts. For a moment he thought that it might be well to accept Marietta's proposition and let Thomas go; but then he remembered the conditions, and he shut his mental eyes at the prospect.

At that moment the gate opened and in walked Thomas Rooper. He had made up his mind and had come to say so; but the sight of the phaeton and gray horse caused him to postpone his intended announcement. "What's Doctor Wicker doin' here?" he asked abruptly.

"Dunno," said Asaph, as carelessly as he could speak. "I don't meddle with household matters of that kind. I expect it's somethin' the matter with that gal Betsey, that Marietta hires to help her. She's always wrong some way or other so that she can't do her own proper work, which I know, havin' to do a good deal of it myself. I expect it's rickets, like as not. Gals do have that sort of thing, don't they?"

"Never had anything to do with sick gals," said Thomas, "or sick people of any sort, and don't want to. But it must be somethin' pretty deep-seated for your sister to send all the way to Timberley for a doctor."

Asaph knew very well that Mrs. Himes was too economical a person to think of doing such a thing as that, and he knew also that Betsey was as good a specimen of rustic health as could be found in the county. And therefore his companion's statement that he wanted to have nothing to do with sick people had for him a saddening import.

"I settled that business of yourn," said Mr. Rooper, "pretty soon after you left me. I thought I might as well come straight around and tell you about it. I'll make you a fair and square offer. I'll give you them clothes, though it strikes me that winter goods will be pretty heavy for this time of year; but it will be on this condition: if I don't get Marietta, you have got to give 'em back."

Asaph smiled.

"I know what you are grinnin' at," said Thomas; "but you needn't think that you are goin' to have the wearin' of them clothes for two or three months and then give 'em back. I don't go in for any long courtships. What I do in that line will be short and sharp."

"How short?" asked Asaph.

"Well, this is Thursday," replied the other, "and I calculate to ask her on Monday."

Asaph looked at his companion in amazement. "By George!" he exclaimed, "that won't work. Why, it took Marietta more'n five days to make up her mind whether she would have the chicken house painted green or red, and you can't expect her to be quicker than that in takin' a new husband. She'd say No just as certain as she would now if you was to go in and ask her right before the doctor and Betsey. And I'll just tell you plain that it wouldn't pay me to do all the hustlin' around and talkin' and argyin' and recommendin' that I'd have to do just for the pleasure of wearin' a suit of warm clothes for four July days. I tell you what it is, it won't do to spring that sort of thing on a woman, especially when she's what you might call a trained widder. You got to give 'em time to think over the matter and to look up your references. There's no use talkin' about it; you must give 'em time, especially when the offer comes from a person that nobody but me has ever thought of as a marryin' man."

"Humph!" said Thomas. "That's all you know about it."

"Facts is facts, and you can't git around 'em. There isn't a woman in this village what wouldn't take at least two weeks to git it into her head that you was really courtin' her. She would be just as likely to think that you was tryin' to git a tenant in place of the McJimseys. But a month of your courtin' and a month of my workin' would just about make the matter all right with Marietta, and then you could sail in and settle it."

"Very good," said Mr. Rooper, rising suddenly. "I will court your sister for one month; and if, on the 17th day of August, she takes me, you can go up to the store and git them clothes; but you can't do it one minute afore. Good mornin'."

Asaph, left alone, heaved a sigh. He did not despair; but truly, fate was heaping a great many obstacles in his path. He thought it was a very hard thing for a man to get his rights in this world.

Mrs. Himes sat on one end of a black hair-covered sofa in the parlor, and Doctor Wicker sat on a black hair-covered chair opposite to her and not far away. The blinds of the window opening upon the garden were drawn up; but those on the front window, which commanded a view of the chestnut tree, were down. Doctor Wicker had just made a proposal of marriage to Mrs. Himes, and at that moment they were both sitting in silence.

The doctor, a bluff, hearty-looking man of about

forty-five, had been very favorably impressed by Mrs. Himes when he first made her acquaintance, during her husband's sickness, and since that time he had seen her occasionally and had thought about her a great deal. Latterly letters had passed between them, and now he had come to make his declaration in person.

It was true, as her brother had said, that Marietta was not quick in making up her mind. But in this case she was able to act more promptly than usual, because she had in a great measure settled this matter before the arrival of the doctor. She knew he was going to propose, and she was very much inclined to accept him. This it was which had made her smile when she was setting the table the afternoon before, and this it was which had prompted her to make her proposition to her brother in regard to his better personal appearance.

But now she was in a condition of nervous trepidation, and made no answer. The doctor thought this was natural enough under the circumstances, but he had no idea of the cause of it. The cause of it was sitting under the chestnut tree, the bright sunlight, streaming through a break in the branches above, illuminating and emphasizing and exaggerating his extreme shabbiness. The doctor had never seen Asaph, and it would have been a great shock to Marietta's self-respect to have him see her brother in his present aspect.

Through a crack in the blind of the front window she had seen Asaph come in and sit down, and she had seen Mr. Rooper arrive and had noticed his departure. And now, with an anxiety which made her chin tremble, she sat and hoped that Asaph would get up and go away. For she knew that if she should say to the doctor what she was perfectly willing to say then and there, he would very soon depart, being a man of practical mind and pressing business; and that, going to the front door with him, she would be obliged to introduce him to a prospective brother-in-law whose appearance, she truly believed, would make him sick. For the doctor was a man, she well knew, who was quite as nice and particular about dress and personal appearance as the late Mr. Himes had been.

Doctor Wicker, aware that the lady's perturbation was increasing instead of diminishing, thought it wise not to press the matter at this moment. He felt that he had been, perhaps, a little over-prompt in making his proposition. "Madam," said he, rising, "I will not ask you to give me an answer now. I will go away and let you think about it, and will come again to-morrow."

Through the crack in the window blind Marietta saw that Asaph was still under the tree. What could she do to delay the doctor? She did not offer to take leave of him, but stood looking upon the floor. It seemed a shame to make so good a man go all the way back to Timberley and come again next day, just because that ragged, dirty Asaph was sitting under the chestnut tree.

The doctor moved toward the door, and as she followed him she glanced once more through the crack in the window blind, and, to her intense delight, she saw Asaph jump up from the bench and run around to the side of the house. He had heard the doctor's footsteps in the hallway and had not wished to meet him. The unsatisfactory condition of his outward appearance had been so strongly impressed upon him of late that he had become a little sensitive in regard to it when strangers were concerned. But if he had only known that his exceedingly unattractive garments had prevented his sister from making a compact which would have totally ruined his plans in regard to her matrimonial disposition and his own advantage, he would have felt for those old clothes the respect and gratitude with which a Roman soldier regarded the shield and sword which had won him a battle.

Down the middle of the garden, at the back of the house, there ran a path, and along this path Asaph walked meditatively, with his hands in his trousers pockets. It was a discouraging place for him to walk, for the beds on each side of him were full of weeds, which he had intended to pull out as soon as he should find time for the work, but which had now grown so tall and strong that they could not be rooted up without injuring the plants, which were the legitimate occupants of the garden.

Asaph did not know it, but at this moment there was not one person in the whole world who thought kindly of him. His sister was so mortified by him that she was in tears in the house. His crony, Thomas, had gone away almost angry with him, and even Betsey, whom he had falsely accused of rickets, and who had often shown a pity for him simply because he looked so forlorn, had steeled her heart against him that morning when she found he had gone away without providing her with any fuel for the kitchen fire.

But he had not made a dozen turns up and down the path before he became aware of the feeling of Marietta. She looked out of the back door and then walked rapidly toward him. "Asaph," said she, "I hope you are considering what I said to you yesterday, for I mean to stick to my word. If you don't choose to accept my offer, I want you to go back to Drummondville early to-morrow morning. And I don't feel in the least as if I were turning you out of the house, for I have given you a chance to stay here, and have only asked you to act like a decent Christian. I will not have you here disgracing my home. When Doctor Wicker came to-day, and I looked out and saw you with that miserable little coat with the sleeves half-way up to the elbows and great holes in it which you will not let anybody patch, because you are too proud to wear patches, and those wretched faded trousers, out at the knees, and which have been turned up and hemmed at the bottom so often that they are six inches above your shoes, and your whole scarecrow appearance, I was so ashamed of you that I could not keep the tears out of my eyes. To tell a respectable gentleman like Doctor Wicker that you were my brother was more than I could bear; and I was glad when I saw you get up and sneak out of the way. I hate to talk to you in this way, Asaph, but you have brought it on yourself."

Her brother looked at her a moment. "Do you want me to go away before breakfast?" he said.

"No," answered Marietta, "but immediately afterward." And in her mind she resolved that breakfast should be very early the next morning.

If Asaph had any idea of yielding, he did not intend to show it until the last moment, and so he changed the subject. "What's the matter with Betsey?" said he. "If she's out of health you'd better get rid of her."

"There's nothing the matter with Betsey," answered his sister. "Doctor Wicker came to see me."

"Came to see you!" exclaimed her brother. "What in the world did he do that for? you never told me that you were ailin'. Is it that sprain in your ankle?"

"Nonsense," said Marietta. "I had almost recovered from that sprain when you came here. There's nothing the matter with my ankle, the trouble is probably with my heart."

The moment she said this she regretted it, for Asaph had so good a head, and could catch meanings so quickly.

"I'm sorry to hear that, Marietta," said Asaph. "That's a good deal more serious."

"Yes," said she. And she turned and went back to the house.

Asaph continued to walk up and down the path. He had not done a stroke of work that morning, but he did not think of that. His sister's communication saddened him. He liked Marietta, and it grieved him to hear that she had anything the matter with her heart. He knew that that often happened to people who looked perfectly well, and there was no reason why he should have suspected any disorder in her. Of course, in this case, there was good reason for her sending for the very best doctor to be had. It was all plain enough to him now.

But as he walked and walked and walked, and looked at the garden, and looked at the little orchard, and looked at the house and the top of the big chestnut tree, which showed itself above the roof, a thought came into his mind which had never been there before — he was Marietta's heir. It was a dreadful thing to think of his sister's possible early departure from this world; but, after all, life is life, reality is reality, and business is business. He was Marietta's only legal heir.

Of course he had known this before, but it had never seemed to be of any importance. He was a good deal older than she was, and he had always looked upon her as a marrying woman. When he made his proposition to Mr. Rooper the thought of his own heirship never came into his mind. In fact, if anyone had offered him ten dollars for said heirship, he would have asked fifteen, and would have afterward agreed to split the difference and take twelve and a half.

But now everything had changed. If Marietta had anything the matter with her heart, there was no knowing when all that he saw might be his own. No sooner had he walked and thought long enough for his mind to fully appreciate the altered aspects of his future, than he determined to instantly thrust out Mr. Rooper from all connection with that future. He would go and tell him so at once.

To the dismay of Betsey, who had been watching him, expecting that he would soon stop walking about and go and saw some wood with which to cook the dinner, he went out of the front gate and strode rapidly into the village. He had some trouble in finding Mr. Rooper, who had gone off to take a walk and arrange a conversation with which to begin his courtship of Mrs. Himes, but he overtook him under a tree by the side of the creek. "Thomas," said he, "I have changed my mind about that business between us. You have been very hard on me, and I'm not goin' to stand it. I can get the clothes and things I need without makin' myself your slave and workin' myself to death, and, perhaps, settin' my sister agin me for life by tryin' to make her believe that black's white, that you are the kind of husband she ought to have, and that you hate pipes and never touch spirits. It would be a mean thing for me to do, and I won't do it. I did think you were a generous-minded man with the right sort of feeling for them as wanted to be your friends, but I have found out that I was mistook, and I'm not goin' to sacrifice my sister to any such person. Now that's my state of mind plain and square."

Thomas Rooper shrunk two inches in height. "Asaph Scantle," he said, in a voice which seemed also to have shrunk, "I don't understand you. I wasn't hard on you. I only wanted to make a fair bargain. If I'd got her, I'd paid up cash on delivery. You couldn't expect a man to do more than that. But I tell you, Asaph, that I am mighty serious about this. The more I have thought about your sister the more I want her. And when I tell you that I've been a-thinkin' about her pretty much all night, you may know that I want her a good deal. And I was intendin' to go to-morrow and begin to court her."

"Well, you needn't," said Asaph. "It won't do no good. If you don't have me to back you up you might as well try to twist that tree as to move her. You can't do it."

"But you don't mean to go agin me, do you, Asaph?" asked Thomas, ruefully.

"'Tain't necessary," replied the other. "You will go agin yourself."

For a few moments Mr. Rooper remained silent. He was greatly discouraged and dismayed by what had been said to him, but he could not yet give up what had become the great object of his life. "Asaph," said he, presently, "it cuts me to the in'ards to think that you have gone back on me; but I tell you what I'll do, if you will promise not to say anything agin me to Mrs. Himes, and not to set yourself in any way between me and her, I'll go along with you to the store now and you can git that suit of clothes and the umbrella, and I'll tell 'em to order the dictionary and hand it over to you as soon as it comes. I'd like you to help me, but if you will only promise to stand out of the way and not hinder, I'll do the fair thing by you and pay in advance."

"Humph!" said Asaph. "I do believe you think you are the only man that wants Marietta."

A pang passed through the heart of Mr. Rooper. He had been thinking a great deal of Mrs. Himes and everything connected with her, and he had even thought of that visit of Doctor Wicker's. That gentleman was a widower and a well-to-do and well-appearing man; and it would have been a long way for him to come just for some trifling rickets in a servant-girl. Being really in love, his imagination was in a very capering mood, and he began to fear that the doctor had come to court Mrs. Himes. "Asaph," he said quickly, "that's a good offer I make you. If you take it, in less than an hour you can walk home looking like a gentleman."

Asaph had taken his reed pipe from his coat pocket and was filling it. As he pushed the coarse tobacco into the bowl, he considered. "Thomas," said he, "that ain't enough. Things have changed, and it wouldn't pay me. But I won't be hard on you. I'm a good friend of yourn, and I'll tell you what I'll do. If you will give me now all the things we spoke of between us, — and I forgot to mention a cane and pocket-handkerchiefs, — and give me, besides, that meerschaum pipe of yourn, I'll promise not to hinder you, but let you go ahead and git Marietta if you kin. I must say it's a good deal for me to do, knowin' how much you'll git and how little you'll give, and knowin', too, the other chances she's got if she wanted 'em; but I'll do it for the sake of friendship."

"My meerschaum pipe!" groaned Mr. Rooper. "My Centennial Exhibition pipe!" His tones were so plaintive that for a moment Asaph felt a little touch of remorse. But then he reflected that if Thomas really did get Marietta the pipe would be of no use to him, for she would not allow him to smoke it. And, besides, realities were realities and business was business. "That pipe may be very dear to you," he said, "Thomas, but I want you to remember that Marietta's very dear to me."

This touched Mr. Rooper, whose heart was sensitive

as it had never been before. "Come along, Asaph," he said. "You shall have everything, meerschaum pipe included. If anybody but me is goin' to smoke that pipe, I'd like it to be my brother-in-law." Thus, with amber-tipped guile, Mr. Rooper hoped to win over his friend to not only not hinder, but to help him.

As the two men walked away, Asaph thought that he was not acting an unfraternal part toward Marietta, for it would not be necessary for him to say or do anything to induce her to refuse so unsuitable a suitor as Thomas Rooper.

About fifteen minutes before dinner — which had been cooked with bits of wood which Betsey had picked up here and there — was ready, Asaph walked into the front yard of his sister's house attired in a complete suit of new clothes, thick and substantial in texture, pepper-and-salt in color, and as long in the legs and arms as the most fastidious could desire. He had on a new shirt and a clean collar, with a handsome black silk cravat tied in a great bow, and a new felt hat was on his head. On his left arm he carried an overcoat, carefully folded, with the lining outside, and in his right hand an umbrella and a cane. In his pockets were half a dozen new handkerchiefs and the case containing Mr. Rooper's Centennial meerschaum.

Marietta, who was in the hallway when he opened the front door, scarcely knew him as he approached.

"Asaph!" she exclaimed. "What has happened to you? Why, you actually look like a gentleman!"

Asaph grinned. "Do you want me to go to Drummondville right after breakfast to-morrow?" he asked.

"My dear brother," said Marietta, "don't crush me by talking about that. But if you could have seen yourself as I saw you, and could have felt as I felt, you would not wonder at me. You must forget all that. I should be proud now to introduce you as my brother to any doctor or king or president. But tell me how you got those beautiful clothes."

Asaph was sometimes beset by an absurd regard for truth, which much annoyed him. He could not say that he had worked for the clothes, and he did not wish his sister to think that he had run in debt for them. "They're paid for, every thread of 'em," he said. "I got 'em in trade. These things is mine, and I don't owe no man a cent for 'em; and it seems to me that dinner must be ready."

"And proud I am," said Marietta, who never before had shown such enthusiastic affection for her brother, "to sit down to the table with such a nice-looking fellow as you are."

The next morning Mr. Rooper came into Mrs. Himes's yard, and there beheld Asaph, in all the glory of his new clothes, sitting under the chestnut tree smoking the Centennial meerschaum pipe. Mr. Rooper himself was dressed in his very best clothes, but he carried with him no pipe.

"Sit down," said Asaph, "and have a smoke."

"No," replied the other; "I am goin' in the house. I have come to see your sister."

"Goin' to begin already?" said Asaph.

"Yes," said the other; "I told you I was going to begin to-day."

"Very good," said his friend, crossing his pepper-

and-salt legs, "and you will finish the 17th of August. That's a good, reasonable time."

But Mr. Rooper had no intention of courting Mrs. Himes for a month. He intended to propose to her that very morning. He had been turning over the matter in his mind, and for several reasons had come to this conclusion. In the first place, he did not believe that he could trust Asaph, even for a single day, not to oppose him. Furthermore, his mind was in such a turmoil from the combined effect of the constantly present thought that Asaph was wearing his clothes, his hat, and his shoes, and smoking his beloved pipe, and of the perplexities and agitations consequent upon his sentiments toward Mrs. Himes, that he did not believe he could bear the mental strain during another night.

Five minutes later Marietta Himes was sitting on the horse-hair sofa in the parlor, with Mr. Rooper on the horse-hair chair opposite to her, and not very far away, and he was delivering the address which he had prepared.

"Madam," said he, "I am a man that takes things in this world as they comes, and is content to wait until the time comes for them to come. I was well acquainted with John Himes. I knowed him in life, and I helped lay him out. As long as there was reason to suppose that the late Mr. Himes — I mean that the grass over the grave of Mr. Himes had remained unwithered, I am not the man to take one step in the direction of his shoes, nor even to consider the size of 'em in connection with the measure of my own feet. But time will pass on in nater as well as in real life; and while I know very well, Mrs. Himes, that certain feelin's towards them that was is like the leaves of the oak tree and can't be blowed off even by the fiercest tempests of affliction, still them leaves will wither in the fall and turn brown and curl up at the edges, though they don't depart, but stick on tight as wax all winter until in the springtime they is pushed off gently without knowin' it by the green leaves which come out in real life as well as nater."

When he had finished this opening Mr. Rooper breathed a little sigh of relief. He had not forgotten any of it, and it pleased him.

Marietta sat and looked at him. She had a good sense of humor and, while she was naturally surprised at what had been said to her, she was greatly amused by it, and really wished to hear what else Thomas Rooper had to say to her.

"Now, madam," he continued, "I am not the man to thrash a tree with a pole to knock the leaves off before their time. But when the young leaves is pushin' and the old leaves is droppin' (not to make any allusion, of course, to any shrivellin' of proper respect), then I come forward, madam, not to take the place of anybody else, but jest as the nateral consequence of the seasons, which everybody ought to expect; even such as you, madam, which I may liken to a hemlock-spruce which keeps straight on in the same general line of appearance without no reference to the fall of the year, nor winter nor summer. And so, Mrs. Himes, I come here to-day to offer to lead you agin to the altar. I have never been there myself, and there ain't no woman in the world that I'd go with but you. I'm a straightforward person, and when I've got a thing to say, I say it, and now I have said it. And so I set here awaitin' your answer."

At this moment the shutters of the front window, which had been closed, were opened, and Asaph put in his head. "Look here, Thomas Rooper," he said, "these shoes is pegged. I didn't bargain for no pegged shoes; I wanted 'em sewed; everything was to be first class."

Mr. Rooper, who had been leaning forward in his chair, his hands upon his knees, and his face glistening with his expressed feelings as brightly as the old-fashioned but shining silk hat which stood on the floor by his side, turned his head, grew red to the ears, and then sprang to his feet. "Asaph Scantle," he cried, with extended fist, "you have broke your word; you hindered."

"No, I didn't," said Asaph, sulkily; "but pegged shoes is too much for any man to stand." And he withdrew from the window, closing the shutters again.

"What does this mean?" asked Mrs. Himes, who had also risen.

"It means," said Thomas, speaking with difficulty, his indignation was so great, "that your brother is a person of tricks and meanders beyond the reach of common human calculation. I don't like to say this of a man who is more or less likely to be my brother-in-law, but I can't help sayin' it, so entirely upset am I at his goin' back on me at such a minute."

"Going back on you?" asked Mrs. Himes. "What do you mean? What has he promised?"

Thomas hesitated. He did not wish to interrupt

his courtship by the discussion of any new question, especially this question. "If we could settle what we have been talkin' about, Mrs. Himes," he said, "and if you would give me my answer, then I could git my mind down to commoner things. But swingin' on a hook as I am, I don't know whether my head or my heels is uppermost, or what's revolvin' around me."

"Oh, I can give you your answer quickly enough," she said. "It is impossible for me to marry you, so that's all settled."

"Impossible is a big word," said Mr. Rooper. "Has anybody else got afore me?"

"I am not bound to answer that question," said Marietta, slightly coloring; "but I cannot accept you, Mr. Rooper."

"Then there's somebody else, of course," said Thomas, gazing darkly upon the floor. "And what's more, Asaph knew it; that's just as clear as daylight. That's what made him come to me yesterday and go back on his first bargain."

"Now then," said Mrs. Himes, speaking very decidedly, "I want to know what you mean by this talk about bargains."

Mr. Rooper knit his brows. "This is mighty different talk," he said, "from the kind I expected when I come here. But you have answered my question, now I'll answer yours. Asaph Scantle, no longer ago than day before yesterday, after hearin' that things wasn't goin' very well with me, recommended me to marry you, and agreed that he would do his level best, by day and by night, to help me git you, if I would give him a suit of clothes, an umbrella, and a dictionary."

At this Mrs. Himes gave a little gasp and sat down.

"Now, I hadn't no thoughts of tradin' for a wife," continued Thomas, "especially in woollen goods and books, but when I considered and turned the matter over in my mind, and thought what a woman you was, and what a life there was afore me if I got you, I agreed to do it. Then he wanted pay aforehand, and that I wouldn't agree to, not because I thought you wasn't wuth it, but because I couldn't trust him if anybody offered him more before I got you. But that ain't the wust of it; yesterday he come down to see me and went back on his bargain, and that, after I had spent the whole night thinkin' of you and what I was goin' to say. And he put on such high-cockalorum airs that I, bein' as soft as mush around the heart, jest wilted and agreed to give him everything he bargained for if he would promise not to hinder. But he wasn't satisfied with that and wouldn't come to no terms until I'd give him my Centennial pipe, what's been like a child to me this many a year. And when he saw how disgruntled I was at sich a loss, he said that my pipe might be very dear to me, but his sister was jest as dear to him. And then, on top of the whole thing, he pokes his head through the shutters and hinders jest at the most ticklish moment."

"A dictionary and a pipe!" ejaculated poor Marietta, her eyes fixed upon the floor.

"But I'm goin' to make him give 'em all back,"

exclaimed Thomas. "They was the price of not hinderin', and he hindered."

"He shall give them back," said Marietta, rising, "but you must understand, Mr. Rooper, that in no way did Asaph interfere with your marrying me. That was a matter with which he did have and could have nothing to do. And now I wish you could get away without speaking to him. I do not want any quarrelling or high words here, and I will see him and arrange the matter better than you can do it."

"Oh, I can git away without speakin' to him," said Mr. Rooper, with reddened face. And so saying, he strode out of the house, through the front yard and out of the gate without turning his head toward Asaph, still sitting under the tree.

"Oh, ho," said the latter to himself, "she's bounced him short and sharp; and it serves him right, too, after playin' that trick on me. Pegged shoes, indeed!"

At this moment the word "Asaph" came from the house in tones shriller and sharper and higher than any in which he had ever heard it pronounced before. He sprang to his feet and went to the house. His sister took him into the parlor and shut the door. Her eyes were red and her face was pale. "Asaph," said she, "Mr. Rooper has told me the whole of your infamous conduct. Now I know what you meant when you said that you were making arrangements to get clothes. You were going to sell me for them. And when you found out that I was likely to marry Doctor Wicker, you put up your price and wanted a dictionary and a pipe."

"No, Marietta," said Asaph, "the dictionary belonged to the first bargain. If you knew how I need a dictionary —"

"Be still!" she cried. "I do not want you to say a word. You have acted most shamefully toward me, and I want you to go away this very day. And before you go you must give back to Mr. Rooper everything that you got from him. I will fit you out with some of Mr. Himes's clothes and make no conditions at all, only that you shall go away. Come up stairs with me, and I will get the clothes."

The room in the garret was opened and various garments which had belonged to the late Mr. Himes were brought out.

"This is pretty hard on me, Marietta," said Asaph, as he held up a coat, "to give up new all-wool goods for things what has been worn and is part cotton, if I am a judge."

Marietta said very little. She gave him what clothes he needed and insisted on his putting them on, making a package of the things he had received from Mr. Rooper and returning them to that gentleman. Asaph at first grumbled, but he finally obeyed with a willingness which might have excited the suspicions of Marietta had she not been so angry.

With an enormous package wrapped in brown paper in one hand and a cane, an umbrella, and a very small hand-bag in the other, Asaph approached the tavern. Mr. Rooper was sitting on the piazza alone. He was smoking a very common-looking clay pipe and gazing intently into the air in front of him. When his old crony came and stood before the piazza he did not turn his head nor his eyes.

"Thomas Rooper," said Asaph, "you have got me into a very bad scrape. I have been turned out of doors on account of what you said about me. And where I am goin' I don't know, for I can't walk to Drummondville. And what's more, I kept my word and you didn't. I didn't hinder you; for how could I suppose that you was goin' to pop the question the very minute you got inside the door? And that dictionary you promised I've not got."

Thomas Rooper answered not a word, but looked steadily in front of him. "And there's another thing," said Asaph. "What are you goin' to allow me for that suit of clothes what I've been wearin', what I took off in your room and left there?"

At this Mr. Rooper sprang to his feet with such violence that the fire danced out of the bowl of his pipe. "What is the fare to Drummondville?" he cried.

Asaph reflected a moment. "Three dollars and fifty cents, includin' supper."

"I'll give you that for them clothes," said the other, and counted out the money.

Asaph took it and sighed. "You've been hard on me, Thomas," said he, "but I bear you no grudge. Good by."

As he walked slowly toward the station Mr. Scantle stopped at the store. "Has that dictionary come that was ordered for me?" he said; and when told that it could not be expected for several days, he did not despair, for it was possible that Thomas Rooper might be so angry that he would forget to countermand the order; in that case he might yet hope to obtain the coveted book.

The package containing the Rooper winter suit was heavy, and Asaph walked slowly. He did not want to go to Drummondville, for he hated book-keeping, and his year of leisure and good living had spoiled him for work and poor fare. In this moody state he was very glad to stop and have a little chat with Mrs. McJimsey, who was sitting at her front window.

This good lady was the principal dressmaker of the village; and by hard work and attention to business she made a very comfortable living. She was a widow, small of stature, thin of feature, very neatly dressed and pleasant to look at. Asaph entered the little front yard, put his package on the doorstep and stood under the window to talk to her. Dressed in the clothes of the late Mr. Himes, her visitor presented such a respectable appearance that Mrs. McJimsey was not in the least ashamed to have people see him standing there, which she would have been a few days ago. Indeed, she felt complimented that he should want to stop. The conversation soon turned upon her removal from her present abode.

"I'm awfully sorry to have to go," she said; "for my time is up just in the middle of my busy season, and that's goin' to throw me back dreadfully. He hasn't done right by me, that Mr. Rooper, in lettin' things go to rack and ruin in this way, and me payin' his rent so regular."

"That's true," said Asaph. "Thomas Rooper is a hard man—a hard man, Mrs. McJimsey. I can see how he would be overbearin' with a lone woman like you: neither your son nor your daughter bein' of age yet to take your part."

"Yes, Mr. Scantle, it's very hard."

Asaph stood for a moment looking at a little bed of zinnias by the side of the doorstep. "What you want, Mrs. McJimsey," said he, "is a man in the house."

In an instant Mrs. McJimsey flushed pink. It was such a strange thing for a gentleman to say to her.

Asaph saw the flush. He had not expected that result from his remark, but he was quick to take advantage of it. "Mrs. McJimsey," said he, "you are a widow, and you are imposed upon, and you need somebody to take care of you. If you will put that job into my hands I will do it. I am a man what works with his head, and if you will let me I'll work for you. To put it square, I ask you to marry me. My sister's goin' to be married, and I'm on the pint of goin' away; for I could not abear to stay in her house when strangers come into it. But if you say the word, I'll stay here and be yours forever and ever more."

Mrs. McJimsey said not a word, but her head drooped and wild thoughts ran through her brain. Thoughts not wild, but well-trained and broken, ran through Asaph's brain. The idea of going to Drummondville and spending for the journey thither a dollar and seventy-five cents of the money he had received from Mr. Rooper now became absolutely repulsive to him.

"Mrs. McJimsey," said he, "I will say more. Not only do I ask you to marry me, but I ask you to do it now. The evenin' sun is settin', the evenin' birds is singin', and it seems to me, Mrs. McJimsey, that all nater pints to this softenin' hour as a marryin' moment. You say your son won't be home from his work until supper time, and your daughter has gone out for a walk. Come with me to Mr. Parker's, the Methodist minister, and let us join hands at the altar there. The gardener and his wife is always ready to stand up as witnesses. And when your son and your daughter comes home to supper, they can find their mother here afore 'em married and settled."

"But, Mr. Scantle," exclaimed Mrs. McJimsey, "it's so suddint. What will the neighbors say?"

"As for bein' suddint, Mrs. McJimsey, I've knowed you for nearly a year, and now, bein' on the way to leave what's been my happy home, I couldn't keep the truth from you no longer. And as for the neighbors, they needn't know that we hain't been engaged for months."

"It's so queer, so very queer," said the little dressmaker. And her face flushed again, and there were tears, not at all sorrowful ones, in her eyes; and her somewhat needle-pricked left hand accidentally laid itself upon the window sill in easy reach of any one outside.

The next morning Mr. Rooper, being of a practical way of thinking, turned his thoughts from love and resentment to the subject of his income. And he soon became convinced that it would be better to keep the McJimseys in his house, if it could be done without too great an outlay for repairs. So he walked over to his property. When he reached the house he was almost stupefied to see Asaph in a chair in the front yard, dressed in the new suit of clothes which he, Thomas Rooper, had paid for, and smoking the Centennial pipe.

"Good morning, Mr. Rooper," said Asaph, in a loud and cheery voice. "I suppose you've come to talk to Mrs. McJimsey about the work you've got to do here to make this house fit to live in. But there ain't no Mrs. McJimsey. She's Mrs. Scantle now, and I'm your tenant. You can talk to me."

Doctor Wicker came to see Mrs. Himes in the afternoon of the day he had promised to come, and early in the autumn they were married. Since Asaph Scantle had married and settled he had not seen his sister nor spoken to her; but he determined that on so joyful an occasion as this he would show no resentment. So he attended the wedding in the village church dressed in the suit of clothes which had belonged to the late Mr. Himes.

MY TERMINAL MORAINE

A MAN'S birth is generally considered the most important event of his existence, but I truly think that what I am about to relate was more important to me than my entrance into this world; because, had not these things happened, I am of the opinion that my life would have been of no value to me and my birth a misfortune.

My father, Joshua Cuthbert, died soon after I came to my majority, leaving me what he had considered a comfortable property. This consisted of a large house and some forty acres of land, nearly the whole of which lay upon a bluff, which upon three sides descended to a little valley, through which ran a gentle stream. I had no brothers or sisters. My mother died when I was a boy, and I, Walter Cuthbert, was left the sole representative of my immediate family.

My estate had been a comfortable one to my father, because his income from the practice of his profession as a physician enabled him to keep it up and provide satisfactorily for himself and me. I had no profession and but a very small income, the result of a few investments my father had made. Left to myself, I felt no inducement to take up any profession or business. My wants were simple, and for a few years I lived without experiencing any inconvenience from the economies which I was obliged to practise. My books, my dog, my gun, and my rod made life pass very pleasantly to me, and the subject of an increase of income never disturbed my mind.

But as time passed on the paternal home began to present an air of neglect and even dilapidation, which occasionally attracted my attention and caused, as I incidentally discovered, a great deal of unfavorable comment among my neighbors, who thought that I should go to work and at least earn money enough to put the house and grounds in a condition which should not be unworthy the memory of the good Dr. Cuthbert. In fact, I began to be looked upon as a shiftless young man; and, now and then, I found a person old enough and bold enough to tell me so.

But, instead of endeavoring to find some suitable occupation by which I might better my condition and improve my estate, I fell in love, which, in the opinion of my neighbors, was the very worst thing that could have happened to me at this time. I lived in a thrifty region, and for a man who could not support himself to think of taking upon him the support of a wife, especially such a wife as Agnes Havelot would be, was considered more than folly and looked upon as a crime. Everybody knew that I was in love with Miss Havelot, for I went to court her as boldly as I went to fish or shoot. There was a good deal of talk about it, and this finally came to the ears of Mr. Havelot, my lady's father, who, thereupon, promptly ordered her to have no more to do with me.

The Havelot estate, which adjoined mine, was a very large one, containing hundreds and hundreds of acres; and the Havelots were rich, rich enough to frighten any poor young man of marrying intent. But I did not appreciate the fact that I was a poor young man. I had never troubled my head about money as it regarded myself, and I now did not trouble my head about it as it regarded Agnes. I loved her, I hoped she loved me, and all other considerations were thrown aside. Mr. Havelot, however, was a man of a different way of thinking.

It was a little time before I became convinced that the decision of Agnes's father, that there should be no communication between that dear girl and myself, really meant anything. I had never been subjected to restrictions, and I did not understand how people of spirit could submit to them; but I was made to understand it when Mr. Havelot, finding me wandering about his grounds, very forcibly assured me that if I should make my appearance there again, or if he discovered any attempt on my part to communicate with his daughter in any way, he would send her from home. He concluded the very brief interview by stating that if I had any real regard for his daughter's happiness I would cease attentions which would meet with the most decided disapprobation from her only surviving parent, and which would result in exiling her from home. I begged for one more interview with Miss Havelot, and if it had been granted I should have assured her of the state of my affections, no matter if there were reasons to suppose that I would never see her again; but her father very sternly forbade anything of the kind, and I went away crushed.

It was a very hard case, for if I played the part of a bold lover, and tried to see Agnes without regard to the wicked orders of her father, I should certainly be discovered; and then it would be not only myself, but the poor girl, who would suffer. So I determined that I would submit to the Havelot decree. No matter if I never saw her again, never heard the sound of her voice, it would be better to have her near me, to have her breathe the same air, cast up her eyes at the same sky, listen to the same birds, that I breathed, looked at, and listened to, than to have her far away, probably in Kentucky, where I knew she had relatives, and where the grass was blue and the sky probably green, or at any rate would appear so to her if in the least degree she felt as I did in regard to the ties of home and the affinities between the sexes.

I now found myself in a most doleful and even desperate condition of mind. There was nothing in the world which I could have for which I cared. Hunting, fishing, and the rambles through woods and fields that had once been so delightful to me, now became tasks which I seldom undertook. The only occupation in which I felt the slightest interest was that of sitting in a tower of my house with a telescope, endeavoring to see my Agnes on some portion of her father's grounds; but, although I diligently directed my glass at the slightest stretch of lawn or bit of path which I could discern through openings in the foliage, I never caught sight of her. I knew, however, by means of daily questions addressed to my cook, whose daughter was a servant in the Havelot house, that Agnes was yet at home. For that reason I remained at home. Otherwise, I should have become a wanderer.

About a month after I had fallen into this most unhappy state an old friend came to see me. We had been school-fellows, but he differed from me in almost every respect. He was full of ambition and energy, and, although he was but a few years older than myself, he had already made a name in the world. He was a geologist, earnest and enthusiastic in his studies and his investigations. He told me frankly that the object of his visit was twofold. In the first place, he wanted to see me, and, secondly, he wanted to make some geological examinations on my grounds, which were situated, as he informed me, upon a terminal moraine, a formation which he had not yet had an opportunity of practically investigating.

I had not known that I lived on a moraine, and now that I knew it, I did not care. But Tom Burton glowed with high spirits and lively zeal as he told me how the great bluff on which my house stood, together with the other hills and wooded terraces which stretched away from it along the side of the valley, had been formed by the minute fragments of rock and soil, which, during ages and ages, had been gradually pushed down from the mountains by a great glacier which once occupied the country to the northeast of my house. "Why, Walter, my boy," he cried, "if I had not read it all in the books I should have known for myself, as soon as I came here, that there had once been a glacier up there, and as it gradually moved to the southwest it had made this country what it is. Have you a stream down there in that dell which I see lies at right-angles with the valley and opens into it?"

"No," said I; "I wish there were one. The only stream we have flows along the valley and not on my property."

Without waiting for me Tom ran down into my dell, pushed his way through the underbrush to its upper end, and before long came back flushed with heat and enthusiasm.

"Well, sir," he said, "that dell was once the bed of a glacial stream, and you may as well clear it out and plant corn there if you want to, for there never will be another stream flowing through it until there is another glacier out in the country beyond. And now I want you to let me dig about here. I want to find out what sort of stuff the glacier brought down from the mountains. I will hire a man and will promise you to fill up all the holes I make."

I had no objection to my friend's digging as much as he pleased, and for three days he busied himself in getting samples of the soil of my estate. Sometimes I went out and looked at him, and gradually a little of his earnest ardor infused itself into me, and with some show of interest I looked into the holes he had made and glanced over the mineral specimens he showed me.

"Well, Walter," said he, when he took leave of me, "I am very sorry that I did not discover that the glacier had raked out the bed of a gold-mine from the mountains up there and brought it down to you, or, at any rate, some valuable iron-ore. But I am obliged to say it did not do anything of the sort. But I can tell you one thing it brought you, and, although it is not of any great commercial value, I should think you could make good use of it here on your place. You have one of the finest deposits of gravel on this bluff that I have met with, and if you were to take out a lot of it and spread it over your driveways and paths, it would make it a great deal pleasanter for you to go about here in bad weather and would wonderfully improve your property. Good roads always give an idea of thrift and prosperity." And then he went away with a valise nearly full of mineral specimens which he assured me were very interesting.

My interest in geological formations died away as soon as Tom Burton had departed, but what he said about making gravel roads giving the place an air of thrift and prosperity had its effect upon my mind. It struck me that it would be a very good thing if people in the neighborhood, especially the Havelots, were to perceive on my place some evidences of thrift and prosperity. Most palpable evidences of unthrift and impecuniosity had cut me off from Agnes, and why might it not be that some signs of improved circumstances would remove, to a degree at least, the restrictions which had been placed between us? This was but a very little thing upon which to build hopes; but ever since men and women have loved they have built grand hopes upon very slight foundations. I determined to put my roadways in order.

My efforts in this direction were really evidence of

anything but thriftiness, for I could not in the least afford to make my drives and walks resemble the smooth and beautiful roads which wound over the Havelot estate, although to do this was my intention, and I set about the work without loss of time. I took up this occupation with so much earnestness that it seriously interfered with my observations from the tower.

I hired two men and set them to work to dig a gravel-pit. They made excavations at several places, and very soon found what they declared to be a very fine quality of road-gravel. I ordered them to dig on until they had taken out what they believed to be enough to cover all my roads. When this had been done, I would have it properly spread and rolled. As this promised to be a very good job, the men went to work in fine spirits and evidently made up their minds that the improvements I desired would require a vast deal of gravel.

When they had dug a hole so deep that it became difficult to throw up the gravel from the bottom, I suggested that they should dig at some other place. But to this they objected, declaring that the gravel was getting better and better, and it would be well to go on down as long as the quality continued to be so good. So, at last, they put a ladder into the pit, one man carrying the gravel up in a hod, while the other dug it; and when they had gone down so deep that this was no longer practicable, they rigged up a derrick and windlass and drew up the gravel in a bucket.

Had I been of a more practical turn of mind I might have perceived that this method of working made the job a very long and, consequently, to the laborers, a profitable one; but no such idea entered into my head, and not noticing whether they were bringing up sand or gravel I allowed them to proceed.

One morning I went out to the spot where the excavation was being made and found that the men had built a fire on the ground near the opening of the pit, and that one of them was bending over it warming himself. As the month was July this naturally surprised me, and I inquired the reason for so strange a performance.

"Upon my soul," said the man who was rubbing his hands over the blaze, "I do not wonder you are surprised, but it's so cold down at the bottom of that pit that me fingers is almost frosted; and we haven't struck any wather neither, which couldn't be expected, of course, a-diggin' down into the hill like this."

I looked into the hole and found it was very deep. "I think it would be better to stop digging here," said I, "and try some other place."

"I wouldn't do that just now," said the other man, who was preparing to go down in the bucket; "to be sure, it's a good deal more like a well than a gravel-pit, but it's bigger at the top than at the bottom, and there's no danger of its cavin' in, and now that we've got everything rigged up all right, it would be a pity to make a change yet awhile."

So I let them go on; but the next day when I went out again I found that they had come to the conclusion that it was time to give up digging in that hole. They both declared that it almost froze their feet to stand on the ground where they worked at the bottom of the excavation. The slow business of drawing up the gravel by means of a bucket and windlass was, therefore, reluctantly given up. The men now went to work to dig outward from this pit toward the edge of the bluff which overlooked my little dell, and gradually made a wide trench, which they deepened until — and I am afraid to say how long they worked before this was done — they could walk to the original pit from the level of the dell. They then deepened the inner end of the trench, wheeling out the gravel in barrows, until they had made an inclined pathway from the dell to the bottom of the pit. The wheeling now became difficult, and the men soon declared that they were sure that they had quite gravel enough.

When they made this announcement, and I had gone into some financial calculations, I found that I would be obliged to put an end to my operations, at least for the present, for my available funds were gone, or would be when I had paid what I owed for the work. The men were very much disappointed by the sudden ending of this good job, but they departed, and I was left to gaze upon a vast amount of gravel of which, for the present at least, I could not afford to make the slightest use.

The mental despondency which had been somewhat lightened during my excavating operations now returned, and I became rather more gloomy and downcast than before. My cook declared that it was of no use to prepare meals which I never ate, and suggested that it would save money if I discharged her. As I had not paid her anything for a long time, I did not see how this would benefit me.

Wandering about one day with my hat pulled down over my eyes and my hands thrust deep into my pockets, I strolled into the dell and stood before the wide trench which led to the pit in which I had foolishly sunk the money which should have supported me for months. I entered this dismal passage and walked slowly and carefully down the incline until I reached the bottom of the original pit, where I had never been before. I stood here looking up and around me and wondering how men could bring themselves to dig down into such dreary depths simply for the sake of a few dollars a week, when I involuntarily began to stamp my feet. They were very cold, although I had not been there more than a minute. I wondered at this and took up some of the loose gravel in my hand. It was quite dry, but it chilled my fingers. I did not understand it, and I did not try to, but walked up the trench and around into the dell thinking of Agnes.

I was very fond of milk, which, indeed, was almost the only food I now cared for, and I was consequently much disappointed at my noonday meal when I found that the milk had soured and was not fit to drink.

"You see, sir," said Susan, "ice is very scarce and dear, and we cannot afford to buy much of it. There was no freezin' weather last winter, and the price has gone up as high as the thermometer, sir, and so, between the two of 'em, I can't keep things from spoilin'."

The idea now came to me that if Susan would take the milk, and anything else she wished to keep cool in this hot weather, to the bottom of the gravel-pit, she would find the temperature there cold enough to preserve them without ice, and I told her so.

The next morning Susan came to me with a pleased countenance and said, "I put the butter and the milk in that pit last night, and the butter's just as hard and the milk's as sweet as if it had been kept in an ice-house. But the place is as cold as an ice-house, sir, and unless I am mistaken, there's ice in it. Anyway, what do you call that?" And she took from a little basket a piece of grayish ice as large as my fist. "When I found it was so cold down there, sir," she said, "I thought I would dig a little myself and see what made it so; and I took a fire-shovel and hatchet and, when I had scraped away some of the gravel, I came to something hard and chopped off this piece of it, which is real ice, sir, or I know nothing about it. Perhaps there used to be an ice-house there, and you might get some of it if you dug, though why anybody should put it down so deep and then cover it up, I'm sure I don't know. But as long as there's any there, I think we should get it out, even if there's only a little of it; for I cannot take everything down to that pit, and we might as well have it in the refrigerator."

This seemed to me like very good sense, and if I had had a man I should have ordered him to go down to the pit and dig up any lumps of ice he might find and bring them to the house. But I had no man, and I therefore became impressed with the opinion that if I did not want to drink sour milk for the rest of the summer, it might be a good thing for me to go down there and dig out some of the ice myself. So with pick-axe and shovel I went to the bottom of the pit and set myself to work.

A few inches below the surface I found that my shovel struck something hard, and, clearing away the gravel from this for two or three square feet, I looked down upon a solid mass of ice. It was dirty and begrimed, but it was truly ice. With my pick I detached some large pieces of it. These, with some discomfort, I carried out into the dell where Susan might come with her basket and get them.

For several days Susan and I took out ice from the pit, and then I thought that perhaps Tom Burton might feel some interest in this frozen deposit in my terminal moraine, and so I wrote to him about it. He did not answer my letter, but instead arrived himself the next afternoon.

"Ice at the bottom of a gravel-pit," said he, "is a thing I never heard of. Will you lend me a spade and a pick-axe?"

When Tom came out of that pit — it was too cold a place for me to go with him and watch his proceedings — I saw him come running toward the house.

"Walter," he shouted, "we must hire all the men we can find and dig, dig, dig. If I am not mistaken something has happened on your place that is wonderful almost beyond belief. But we must not stop to talk. We must dig, dig, dig; dig all day and dig all night. Don't think of the cost. I'll attend to that. I'll get the money. What we must do is to find men and set them to work."

"What's the matter?" said I. "What has happened?"

"I haven't time to talk about it now; besides I don't want to, for fear that I should find that I am mistaken. But get on your hat, my dear fellow, and let's go over to the town for men."

The next day there were eight men working under the direction of my friend Burton, and although they did not work at night as he wished them to do, they labored steadfastly for ten days or more before Tom was ready to announce what it was he had hoped to discover, and whether or not he had found it. For a day or two I watched the workmen from time to time, but after that I kept away, preferring to await the result of my friend's operations. He evidently expected to find something worth having, and whether he was successful or not, it suited me better to know the truth all at once and not by degrees.

On the morning of the eleventh day Tom came into the room where I was reading and sat down near me. His face was pale, his eyes glittering. "Old friend," said he, and as he spoke I noticed that his voice was a little husky, although it was plain enough that his emotion was not occasioned by bad fortune—"my good old friend, I have found out what made the bottom of your gravel-pit so uncomfortably cold. You need not doubt what I am going to tell you, for my excavations have been complete and thorough enough to make me sure of what I say. Don't you remember that I told you that ages ago there was a vast glacier in the country which stretches from here to the mountains? Well, sir, the foot of that glacier must have reached further this way than is generally supposed. At any rate a portion of it did extend in this direction as far as this bit of the world which is now yours. This end, or spur of the glacier, nearly a quarter of a mile in width, I should say, and pushing before it a portion of the terminal moraine on which you live, came slowly toward the valley until suddenly it detached itself from the main glacier and disappeared from sight. That is to say, my boy" — and as he spoke Tom sprang to his feet, too excited to sit any longer — "it descended to the bowels of the earth, at least for a considerable distance in that direction. Now you want to know how this happened. Well, I'll tell you. In this part of the country there are scattered about here and there great caves. Geologists know one or two of them, and it is certain that there are others undiscovered. Well, sir, your glacier spur discovered one of them, and when it had lain over the top of it for an age or two, and had grown bigger and bigger, and heavier and heavier, it at last burst through the rock roof of the cave, snapping itself from the rest of the glacier and falling in one vast mass to the bottom of the subterranean abyss. Walter, it is there now. The rest of the glacier came steadily down; the moraines were forced before it; they covered up this glacier spur, this broken fragment, and by the time the climate changed and the average of temperature rose above that of the glacial period, this vast sunken mass of ice was packed away below the surface of the earth, out of the reach of the action of friction, or heat, or moisture, or anything else which might destroy it. And through all the long procession of centuries that broken end of the glacier has been lying in your terminal moraine. It is there now. It is yours, Walter Cuthbert. It is an ice-mine. It is wealth, and so far as I can make out, it is nearly all upon your land. To you is the possession, but to me is the glory of the discovery. A bit of the glacial period kept in a cave for us! It is too wonderful to believe! Walter, have you any brandy?"

It may well be supposed that by this time I was thoroughly awakened to the importance and the amazing character of my friend's discovery, and I hurried with him to the scene of operations. There he explained everything and showed me how, by digging away a portion of the face of the bluff, he had found that this vast fragment of the glacier, which had been so miraculously preserved, ended in an irregularly perpendicular wall, which extended downward he knew not how far, and the edge of it on its upper side had been touched by my workmen in digging their pit. "It was the gradual melting of the upper end of this glacier," said Tom, "probably more elevated than the lower end, that made your dell. I wondered why the depression did not extend further up toward the spot where the foot of the glacier was supposed to have been. This end of the fragment, being sunk in deeper and afterward covered up more completely, probably never melted at all."

"It is amazing — astounding," said I; "but what of it, now that we have found it?"

"What of it?" cried Tom, and his whole form trembled as he spoke. "You have here a source of wealth, of opulence which shall endure for the rest of your days. Here at your very door, where it can be taken out and transported with the least possible trouble, is ice enough to supply the town, the county, yes, I might say, the State, for hundreds of years.

No, sir; I cannot go in to supper. I cannot eat. I leave to you the business and practical part of this affair. I go to report upon its scientific features."

"Agnes," I exclaimed, as I walked to the house with my hands clasped and my eyes raised to the sky, "the glacial period has given thee to me!"

This did not immediately follow, although I went that very night to Mr. Havelot and declared to him that I was now rich enough to marry his daughter. He laughed at me in a manner which was very annoying, and made certain remarks which indicated that he thought it probable that it was not the roof of the cave, but my mind, which had given away under the influence of undue pressure.

The contemptuous manner in which I had been received aroused within me a very unusual state of mind. While talking to Mr. Havelot I heard not far away in some part of the house a voice singing. It was the voice of Agnes, and I believed she sang so that I could hear her. But as her sweet tones reached my ear there came to me at the same time the harsh, contemptuous words of her father. I left the house determined to crush that man to the earth beneath a superincumbent mass of ice — or the evidence of the results of the ownership of such a mass — which would make him groan and weep as he apologized to me for his scornful and disrespectful utterances and at the same time offered me the hand of his daughter.

When the discovery of the ice-mine, as it grew to be called, became generally known my grounds were crowded by sight-seers, and reporters of newspapers were more plentiful than squirrels. But the latter were referred to Burton, who would gladly talk to them as long as they could afford to listen, and I felt myself at last compelled to shut my gates to the first.

I had offers of capital to develop this novel source of wealth, and I accepted enough of this assistance to enable me to begin operations on a moderate scale. It was considered wise not to uncover any portion of the glacier spur, but to construct an inclined shaft down to its wall-like end, and from this tunnel into the great mass. Immediately the leading ice company of the neighboring town contracted with me for all the ice I could furnish, and the flood-gates of affluence began slowly to rise.

The earliest, and certainly one of the greatest, benefits which came to me from this bequest from the unhistoric past was the new energy and vigor with which my mind and body were now infused. My old, careless method of life and my recent melancholy, despairing mood were gone, and I now began to employ myself upon the main object of my life with an energy and enthusiasm almost equal to that of my friend Tom Burton. This present object of my life was to prepare my home for Agnes.

The great piles of gravel which my men had dug from the well-like pit were spread upon the roadways and rolled smooth and hard; my lawn was mowed; my flower-beds and borders put in order; useless bushes and undergrowth cut out and cleared away; my out-buildings were repaired, and the grounds around my house rapidly assumed their old appearance of neatness and beauty. Ice was very scarce that summer, and, as the wagons wound away from the opening of the shaft which led down to the glacier, carrying their loads to the nearest railway-station, so money came to me; not in large sums at first, for preparations had not yet been perfected for taking out the ice in great quantities, but enough to enable me to go on with my work as rapidly as I could plan it. I set about renovating and brightening and newly furnishing my house. Whatever I thought that Agnes would like I bought and put into it. I tried to put myself in her place as I selected the paper-hangings and the materials with which to cover the furniture.

Sometimes, while thus employed selecting ornaments or useful articles for my house, and using as far as was possible the taste and judgment of another instead of my own, the idea came to me that perhaps Agnes had never heard of my miraculous good fortune. Certainly her father would not be likely to inform her, and perhaps she still thought of me, if she thought at all, as the poor young man from whom she had been obliged to part because he was poor.

But whether she knew that I was growing rich, or whether she thought I was becoming poorer and poorer, I thought only of the day when I could go to her father and tell him that I was able to take his daughter and place her in a home as beautiful as that in which she now lived, and maintain her with all the comforts and luxuries which he could give her.

One day I asked my faithful cook, who also acted as my housekeeper and general supervisor, to assist me in making out a list of china which I intended to purchase.

"Are you thinking of buying china, sir?" she

asked. "We have now quite as much as we really need."

"Oh, yes," said I, "I shall get complete sets of everything that can be required for a properly furnished household."

Susan gave a little sigh. "You are spendin' a lot of money, sir, and some of it for things that a single gentleman would be likely not to care very much about; and if you was to take it into your head to travel and stay away for a year or two, there's a good many things you've bought that would look shabby when you come back, no matter how careful I might be in dustin' 'em and keepin' 'em covered."

"But I have no idea of travelling," said I. "There's no place so pleasant as this to me."

Susan was silent for a few moments, and then she said: "I know very well why you are doing all this, and I feel it my bounden duty to say to you that there's a chance of its bein' no use. I do not speak without good reason, and I would not do it if I didn't think that it might make trouble lighter to you when it comes."

"What are you talking about, Susan? what do you mean?"

"Well, sir, this is what I mean: It was only last night that my daughter Jane was in Mr. Havelot's dining-room after dinner was over, and Mr. Havelot and a friend of his were sitting there, smoking their cigars and drinking their coffee. She went in and come out again as she was busy takin' away the dishes, and they paid no attention to her, but went on talkin' without knowing, most likely, she was there. Mr. Havelot and the gentleman were talkin' about you, and Jane she heard Mr. Havelot say as plain as anything, and she said she couldn't be mistaken, that even if your nonsensical ice-mine proved to be worth anything, he would never let his daughter marry an iceman. He spoke most disrespectful of icemen, sir, and said that it would make him sick to have a son-in-law whose business it was to sell ice to butchers, and hotels, and grog-shops, and pork-packers, and all that sort of people; and that he would as soon have his daughter marry the man who supplied a hotel with sausages as the one who supplied it with ice to keep those sausages from spoiling. You see, sir, Mr. Havelot lives on his property as his father did before him, and he is a very proud man, with a heart as hard and cold as that ice down under your hand; and it's borne in on me very strong, sir, that it would be a bad thing for you to keep on thinkin' that you are gettin' this house all ready to bring Miss Havelot to when you have married her. For if Mr. Havelot keeps on livin', which there's every chance of his doin', it may be many a weary year before you get Miss Agnes, if you ever get her. And havin' said that, sir, I say no more, and I would not have said this much if I hadn't felt it my bounden duty to your father's son to warn him that most likely he was workin' for what he might never get, and so keep him from breakin' his heart when he found out the truth all of a sudden."

With that Susan left me, without offering any assistance in making out a list of china. This was a terrible story; but, after all, it was founded only upon servants' gossip. In this country even proud, rich men like Mr. Havelot did not have such absurd ideas regarding the source of wealth. Money is money, and whether it is derived from the ordinary products of the earth, from which came much of Mr. Havelot's revenue, or from an extraordinary project such as my glacier spur, it truly could not matter so far as concerned the standing in society of its possessor. What utter absurdity was this which Susan had told me! If I were to go to Mr. Havelot and tell him that I would not marry his daughter because he supplied brewers and bakers with the products of his fields, would he not consider me an idiot? I determined to pay no attention to the idle tale. But, alas! determinations of that sort are often of little avail. I did pay attention to it, and my spirits drooped.

The tunnel into the glacier spur had now attained considerable length, and the ice in the interior was found to be of a much finer quality than that first met with, which was of a grayish hue and somewhat inclined to crumble. When the workmen reached a grade of ice as good as they could expect, they began to enlarge the tunnel into a chamber, and from this they proposed to extend tunnels in various directions after the fashion of a coal-mine. The ice was hauled out on sledges through the tunnel and then carried up a wooden railway to the mouth of the shaft.

It was comparatively easy to walk down the shaft and enter the tunnel, and when it happened that the men were not at work I allowed visitors to go down and view this wonderful ice-cavern. The walls of the chamber appeared semi-transparent, and the light of the candles or lanterns gave the whole scene a weird and beautiful aspect. It was almost possible to imagine oneself surrounded by limpid waters, which might at any moment rush upon him and engulf him.

Every day or two Tom Burton came with a party of scientific visitors, and had I chosen to stop the work of taking out ice, admitted the public and charged a price for admission, I might have made almost as much money as I at that time derived from the sale of the ice. But such a method of profit was repugnant to me.

For several days after Susan's communication to me, I worked on in my various operations, endeavoring to banish from my mind the idle nonsense she had spoken of; but one of its effects upon me was to make me feel that I ought not to allow hopes so important to rest upon uncertainties. So I determined that as soon as my house and grounds should be in a condition with which I should for the time be satisfied, I would go boldly to Mr. Havelot, and, casting out of my recollection everything that Susan had said, invite him to visit me and see for himself the results of the discovery of which he had spoken with such derisive contempt. This would be a straightforward and business-like answer to his foolish objections to me, and I believed that in his heart the old gentleman would properly appreciate my action.

About this time there came to my place Aaron Boyce, an elderly farmer of the neighborhood, and, finding me outside, he seized the opportunity to have a chat with me.

"I tell you what it is, Mr. Cuthbert," said he, "the people in this neighborhood hasn't give you credit for what's in you. The way you have fixed up this place, and the short time you have took to do it, is enough to show us now what sort of a man you are; and I tell you, sir, we're proud of you for a neighbor. I don't believe there's another gentleman in this county of your age that could have done what you have done in so short a time. I expect now you will be thinking of getting married and startin' housekeepin' in a regular fashion. That comes just as natural as to set hens in the spring. By the way, have you heard that old Mr. Havelot's thinkin' of goin' abroad? I didn't believe he would ever do that again, because he's gettin' pretty well on in years, but old men will do queer things as well as young ones."

"Going abroad!" I cried. "Does he intend to take his daughter with him?"

Mr. Aaron Boyce smiled grimly. He was a great old gossip, and he had already obtained the information he wanted. "Yes," he said, "I've heard it was on her account he's going. She's been kind of weakly lately, they tell me, and hasn't took to her food, and the doctors has said that what she wants is a sea-voyage and a change to foreign parts."

Going abroad! Foreign parts! This was more terrible than anything I had imagined. I would go to Mr. Havelot that very evening, the only time which I would be certain to find him at home, and talk to him in a way which would be sure to bring him to his senses, if he had any. And if I should find that he had no sense of propriety or justice, no sense of his duty to his fellow-man and to his offspring, then I would begin a bold fight for Agnes, a fight which I would not give up until, with her own lips, she told me that it would be useless. I would follow her to Kentucky, to Europe, to the uttermost ends of the earth. I could do it now. The frozen deposits in my terminal moraine would furnish me with the means. I walked away and left the old farmer standing grinning. No doubt my improvements and renovations had been the subject of gossip in the neighborhood, and he had come over to see if he could find out anything definite in regard to the object of them. He had succeeded, but he had done more: he had nerved me to instantly begin the conquest of Agnes, whether by diplomacy or war.

I was so anxious to begin this conquest that I could scarcely wait for the evening to come. At the noon-hour, when the ice-works were deserted, I walked down the shaft and into the ice-chamber to see what had been done since my last visit. I decided to insist that operations upon a larger scale should be immediately begun, in order that I might have plenty of money with which to carry on my contemplated campaign. Whether it was one of peace or war, I should want all the money I could get.

I took with me a lantern and went around the chamber, which was now twenty-five or thirty feet in diameter, examining the new inroads which had been made upon its walls. There was a tunnel commenced opposite the one by which the chamber was entered, but it had not been opened more than a dozen feet, and it seemed to me that the men had not been working with any very great energy. I wanted to see a continuous stream of ice-blocks from that chamber to the mouth of the shaft.

While grumbling thus I heard behind me a sudden noise like thunder and the crashing of walls, and, turning quickly, I saw that a portion of the roof of the chamber had fallen in. Nor had it ceased to fall. As I gazed several great masses of ice came down from above and piled themselves upon that which had already fallen.

Startled and frightened, I sprang toward the opening of the entrance tunnel; but, alas! I found that that was the point where the roof had given away, and between me and the outer world was a wall of solid ice through which it would be as impossible for me to break as if it were a barrier of rock. With the quick instinct which comes to men in danger I glanced about to see if the workmen had left their tools; but there were none. They had been taken outside. Then I stood and gazed stupidly at the mass of fallen ice, which, even as I looked upon it, was cracking and snapping, pressed down by the weight above it, and forming itself into an impervious barrier without crevice or open seam.

Then I madly shouted. But of what avail were shouts down there in the depths of the earth? I soon ceased this useless expenditure of strength, and, with my lantern in my hand, began to walk around the chamber, throwing the light upon the walls and the roof. I became impressed with the fear that the whole cavity might cave in at once and bury me here in a tomb of ice. But I saw no cracks, nor any sign of further disaster. But why think of anything more? Was not this enough? For, before that ice-barrier could be cleared away, would I not freeze to death?

I now continued to walk, not because I expected to find anything or do anything, but simply to keep myself warm by action. As long as I could move about I believed that there was no immediate danger of succumbing to the intense cold; for, when a young man, travelling in Switzerland, I had been in the cave of a glacier, and it was not cold enough to prevent some old women from sitting there to play the zither for the sake of a few coppers from visitors. I could not expect to be able to continue walking until I should be rescued, and if I sat down, or by chance slept from exhaustion, I must perish.

The more I thought of it, the more sure I became that in any case I must perish. A man in a block of ice could have no chance of life. And Agnes! Oh, Heavens! what demon of the ice had leagued with old Havelot to shut me up in this frozen prison? For a long time I continued to walk, beat my body with my arms, and stamp my feet. The instinct of life was strong within me. I would live as long as I could, and think of Agnes. When I should be frozen I could not think of her.

Sometimes I stopped and listened. I was sure I could hear noises, but I could not tell whether they were above me or not. In the centre of the ice-barrier, about four feet from the ground, was a vast block of the frozen substance which was unusually clear and seemed to have nothing on the other side of it; for through it I could see flickers of light, as though people were going about with lanterns. It was quite certain that the accident had been discovered; for, had not the thundering noise been heard by persons outside, the workmen would have seen what had happened as soon as they came into the tunnel to begin their afternoon operations.

At first I wondered why they did not set to work with a will and cut away this barrier and let me out. But there suddenly came to my mind a reason for this lack of energy which was more chilling than the glistening walls around me: Why should they suppose that I was in the ice-chamber? I was not in the habit of coming here very often, but I was in the habit of wandering off by myself at all hours of the day. This thought made me feel that I might as well lie down on the floor of this awful cave and die at once. The workmen might think it unsafe to mine any further in this part of the glacier, and begin operations at some other point. I did sit down for a moment, and then I rose involuntarily and began my weary round. Suddenly I thought of looking at my watch. It was nearly five o'clock. I had been more than four hours in that dreadful place, and I did not believe that I could continue to exercise my limbs very much longer. The lights I had seen had ceased. It was quite plain that the workmen had no idea that any one was imprisoned in the cave.

But soon after I had come to this conclusion I saw through the clear block of ice a speck of light, and it became stronger and stronger, until I believed it to be close to the other side of the block. There it remained stationary; but there seemed to be other points of light which moved about in a strange way, and near it. Now I stood by the block watching. When my feet became very cold, I stamped them; but there I stood fascinated, for what I saw was truly surprising. A large coal of fire appeared on the other side of the block; then it suddenly vanished and was succeeded by another coal. This disappeared, and another took its place, each one seeming to come nearer and nearer to me. Again and again did these coals appear. They reached the centre of the block; they approached my side of it. At last one was so near to me that I thought it was about to break through, but it vanished. Then there came a few quick thuds and the end of a piece of iron protruded from the block. This was withdrawn, and through the aperture there came a voice which said: "Mr. Cuthbert, are you in there?" It was the voice of Agnes!

Weak and cold as I was, fire and energy rushed through me at these words. "Yes," I exclaimed, my mouth to the hole; "Agnes, is that you?"

"Wait a minute," came from the other side of the aperture. "I must make it bigger. I must keep it from closing up."

Again came the coals of fire, running backward and forward through the long hole in the block of ice. I could see now what they were. They were irons used by plumbers for melting solder and that sort of thing, and Agnes was probably heating them in a little furnace outside, and withdrawing them as fast as they cooled. It was not long before the aperture was very much enlarged; and then there came grating through it a long tin tube nearly two inches in diameter, which almost, but not quite, reached my side of the block.

Now came again the voice of Agnes: "Oh, Mr. Cuthbert, are you truly there? Are you crushed? Are you wounded? Are you nearly frozen? Are you starved? Tell me quickly if you are yet safe."

Had I stood in a palace padded with the softest silk and filled with spicy odors from a thousand rose-gardens, I could not have been better satisfied with my surroundings than I was at that moment. Agnes was not two feet away! She was telling me that she cared for me! In a very few words I assured her that I was uninjured. Then I was on the point of telling her I loved her, for I believed that not a moment should be lost in making this avowal. I could not die without her knowing that. But the appearance of a mass of paper at the other end of the tube prevented the expression of my sentiments. This was slowly pushed on until I could reach it. Then there came the words: "Mr. Cuthbert, these are sandwiches. Eat them immediately and walk about while you are doing it. You must keep yourself warm until the men get to you."

Obedient to the slightest wish of this dear creature, I went twice around the cave, devouring the sandwiches as I walked. They were the most delicious food that I had ever tasted. They were given to me by Agnes. I came back to the opening. I could not immediately begin my avowal. I must ask a question first. "Can they get to me?" I inquired. "Is anybody trying to do that? Are they working there by you? I do not hear them at all."

"Oh, no," she answered; "they are not working here. They are on top of the bluff, trying to dig down to you. They were afraid to meddle with the ice here for fear that more of it might come down and crush you and the men, too. Oh, there has been a dreadful excitement since it was found that you were in there!"

"How could they know I was here?" I asked.

"It was your old Susan who first thought of it. She saw you walking toward the shaft about noon, and then she remembered that she had not seen you again; and when they came into the tunnel here they found one of the lanterns gone and the big stick you generally carry lying where the lantern had been. Then it was known that you must be inside. Oh, then there was an awful time! The foreman of the icemen examined everything, and said they must dig down to you from above. He put his men to work; but they could do very little, for they had hardly any spades. Then they sent into town for help and over to the new park for the Italians working there. From the way these men set to work you might have thought that they would dig away the whole bluff in about five minutes; but they didn't. Nobody seemed to know what to do, or how to get to work; and the hole they made when they did begin was filled up with men almost as fast as they threw out the stones and gravel. I don't believe anything would have been done properly if your friend, Mr. Burton, hadn't happened to come with two scientific gentlemen, and since that he has been directing everything. You can't think what a splendid fellow he is! I fairly adored him when I saw him giving his orders and making everybody skip around in the right way."

"Tom is a very good man," said I; "but it is his business to direct that sort of work, and it is not surprising that he knows how to do it. But, Agnes, they may never get down to me, and we do not know that this roof may not cave in upon me at any moment; and before this or anything else happens I want to tell you —"

"Mr. Cuthbert," said Agnes, "is there plenty of oil in your lantern? It would be dreadful if it were to go out and leave you there in the dark. I thought of that and brought you a little bottle of kerosene so that you can fill it. I am going to push the bottle through now, if you please." And with this a large phial, cork-end foremost, came slowly through the tube, propelled by one of the soldering-irons. Then came Agnes's voice: "Please fill your lantern immediately, because if it goes out you cannot find it in the dark; and then walk several times around the cave, for you have been standing still too long already."

I obeyed these injunctions, but in two or three minutes was again at the end of the tube. "Agnes," said I, "how did you happen to come here? Did you contrive in your own mind this method of communicating with me?"

"Oh, yes; I did," she said. "Everybody said that this mass of ice must not be meddled with, but I knew very well it would not hurt it to make a hole through it."

"But how did you happen to be here?" I asked.

"Oh, I ran over as soon as I heard of the accident.

Everybody ran here. The whole neighborhood is on top of the bluff; but nobody wanted to come into the tunnel, because they were afraid that more of it might fall in. So I was able to work here all by myself, and I am very glad of it. I saw the soldering-iron and the little furnace outside of your house where the plumbers had been using them, and I brought them here myself. Then I thought that a simple hole through the ice might soon freeze up again, and if you were alive inside I could not do anything to help you; and so I ran home and got my diploma-case, that had had one end melted out of it, and I brought that to stick in the hole. I'm so glad that it is long enough, or almost."

"Oh, Agnes," I cried, "you thought of all this for me?"

"Why, of course, Mr. Cuthbert," she answered, before I had a chance to say anything more. "You were in great danger of perishing before the men got to you, and nobody seemed to think of any way to give you immediate relief. And don't you think that a collegiate education is a good thing for girls—at least, that it was for me?"

"Agnes," I exclaimed; "please let me speak. I want to tell you, I must tell you—"

But the voice of Agnes was clearer than mine and it overpowered my words. "Mr. Cuthbert," she said, "we cannot both speak through this tube at the same time in opposite directions. I have here a bottle of water for you, but I am very much afraid it will not go through the diploma-case."

"Oh, I don't want any water," I said. "I can

eat ice if I am thirsty. What I want is to tell you—"

"Mr. Cuthbert," said she, "you must not eat that ice. Water that was frozen countless ages ago may be very different from the water of modern times, and might not agree with you. Don't touch it, please. I am going to push the bottle through if I can. I tried to think of everything that you might need and brought them all at once; because, if I could not keep the hole open, I wanted to get them to you without losing a minute."

Now the bottle came slowly through. It was a small beer-bottle, I think, and several times I was afraid it was going to stick fast and cut off communication between me and the outer world; that is to say, between me and Agnes. But at last the cork and the neck appeared, and I pulled it through. I did not drink any of it, but immediately applied my mouth to the tube.

"Agnes," I said; "my dear Agnes, really you must not prevent me from speaking. I cannot delay another minute. This is an awful position for me to be in, and as you don't seem to realize—"

"But I do realize, Mr. Cuthbert, that if you don't walk about you will certainly freeze before you can be rescued. Between every two or three words you want to take at least one turn around that place. How dreadful it would be if you were suddenly to become benumbed and stiff! Everybody is thinking of that. The best diggers that Mr. Burton had were three colored men; but after they had gone down nothing like as deep as a well, they came up frightened and said they would not dig another shovelful for the whole world. Perhaps you don't know it, but there's a story about the neighborhood that the negro hell is under your property. You know many of the colored people expect to be everlastingly punished with ice and not with fire —"

"Agnes," I interrupted, "I am punished with ice and fire both. Please let me tell you —"

"I was going on to say, Mr. Cuthbert," she interrupted, "that when the Italians heard why the colored men had come out of the hole they would not go in either, for they are just as afraid of everlasting ice as the negroes are, and were sure that if the bottom came out of that hole they would fall into a frozen lower world. So there was nothing to do but to send for paupers, and they are working now. You know paupers have to do what they are told without regard to their beliefs. They got a dozen of them from the poorhouse. Somebody said they just threw them into the hole. Now I must stop talking, for it is time for you to walk around again. Would you like another sandwich?"

"Agnes," said I, endeavoring to speak calmly, "all I want is to be able to tell you —"

"And when you walk, Mr. Cuthbert, you had better keep around the edge of the chamber, for there is no knowing when they may come through. Mr. Burton and the foreman of the icemen measured the bluff so that they say the hole they are making is exactly over the middle of the chamber you are in, and if you walk around the edge the pieces may not fall on you."

"If you don't listen to me, Agnes," I said, "I'll

go and sit anywhere, everywhere, where death may come to me quickest. Your coldness is worse than the coldness of the cave. I cannot bear it."

"But, Mr. Cuthbert," said Agnes, speaking, I thought, with some agitation, "I have been listening to you, and what more can you possibly have to say? If there is anything you want, let me know. I will run and get it for you."

"There is no need that you should go away to get what I want," I said. "It is there with you. It is you."

"Mr. Cuthbert," said Agnes, in a very low voice, but so distinctly that I could hear every word, "don't you think it would be better for you to give your whole mind to keeping yourself warm and strong? For if you let yourself get benumbed you may sink down and freeze."

"Agnes," I said, "I will not move from this little hole until I have told you that I love you, that I have no reason to care for life or rescue unless you return my love, unless you are willing to be mine. Speak quickly to me, Agnes, because I may not be rescued and may never know whether my love for you is returned or not."

At this moment there was a tremendous crash behind me, and, turning, I saw a mass of broken ice upon the floor of the cave, with a cloud of dust and smaller fragments still falling. And then with a great scratching and scraping, and a howl loud enough to waken the echoes of all the lower regions, down came a red-headed, drunken shoemaker. I cannot say that he was drunk at that moment, but I knew the man the moment I saw his carroty poll, and it was drink which had sent him to the poorhouse.

But the sprawling and howling cobbler did not reach the floor. A rope had been fastened around his waist to prevent a fall in case the bottom of the pit should suddenly give way, and he hung dangling in mid-air with white face and distended eyes, cursing and swearing and vociferously entreating to be pulled up. But before he received any answer from above, or I could speak to him, there came through the hole in the roof of the cave a shower of stones and gravel, and with them a frantic Italian, his legs and arms outspread, his face wild with terror.

Just as he appeared in view he grasped the rope of the cobbler, and, though in a moment he came down heavily upon the floor of the chamber, this broke his fall, and he did not appear to be hurt. Instantly he crouched low and almost upon all fours, and began to run around the chamber, keeping close to the walls and screaming, I suppose, to his saints to preserve him from the torments of the frozen damned.

In the midst of this hubbub came the voice of Agnes through the hole: "Oh, Mr. Cuthbert, what has happened? Are you alive?"

I was so disappointed by the appearance of these wretched interlopers at the moment it was about to be decided whether my life — should it last for years, or but for a few minutes — was to be black or bright, and I was so shaken and startled by the manner of their entry upon the scene, that I could not immediately shape the words necessary to inform Agnes what had happened. But, collecting my faculties, I was about to speak, when suddenly, with the force of the hind leg of a mule, I was pushed away from the aperture, and the demoniac Italian clapped his great mouth to the end of the tube and roared through it a volume of oaths and supplications. I attempted to thrust aside the wretched being, but I might as well have tried to move the ice-barrier itself. He had perceived that some one outside was talking to me, and in his frenzy he was imploring that some one should let him out.

While still endeavoring to move the man, I was seized by the arm, and turning, beheld the pallid face of the shoemaker. They had let him down so that he reached the floor. He tried to fall on his knees before me, but the rope was so short that he was able to go only part of the way down, and presented a most ludicrous appearance, with his toes scraping the icy floor and his arms thrown out as if he were paddling like a tadpole. "Oh, have mercy upon me, sir," he said, "and help me get out of this dreadful place. If you go to the hole and call up it's you, they will pull me up; but if they get you out first they will never think of me. I am a poor pauper, sir, but I never did nothin' to be packed in ice before I am dead."

Noticing that the Italian had left the end of the aperture in the block of ice, and that he was now shouting up the open shaft, I ran to the channel of communication which my Agnes had opened for me, and called through it; but the dear girl had gone.

The end of a ladder now appeared at the opening in the roof; and this was let down until it reached the floor. I started toward it, but before I had gone half the distance the frightened shoemaker and the maniac Italian sprang upon it, and, with shrieks and oaths, began a maddening fight for possession of the ladder. They might quickly have gone up one after the other, but each had no thought but to be first; and as one seized the rounds he was pulled away by the other, until I feared the ladder would be torn to pieces. The shoemaker finally pushed his way up a little distance, when the Italian sprang upon his back, endeavoring to climb over him; and so on they went up the shaft, fighting, swearing, kicking, scratching, shaking and wrenching the ladder, which had been tied to another one in order to increase its length, so that it was in danger of breaking, and tearing at each other in a fashion which made it wonderful that they did not both tumble headlong downward. They went on up, so completely filling the shaft with their struggling forms and their wild cries that I could not see or hear anything, and was afraid, in fact, to look up toward the outer air.

As I was afterward informed, the Italian, who had slipped into the hole by accident, ran away like a frightened hare the moment he got his feet on firm ground, and the shoemaker sat down and swooned. By this performance he obtained from a benevolent bystander a drink of whiskey, the first he had had since he was committed to the poorhouse.

But a voice soon came down the shaft calling to me. I recognized it as that of Tom Burton, and replied that I was safe, and that I was coming up the ladder. But in my attempt to climb, I found that I was unable to do so. Chilled and stiffened by the cold and weakened by fatigue and excitement, I believe I never should have been able to leave that ice-chamber if my faithful friend had not come down the ladder and vigorously assisted me to reach the outer air.

Seated on the ground, my back against a great oak-tree, I was quickly surrounded by a crowd of my neighbors, the workmen, and the people who had been drawn to the spot by the news of the strange accident to gaze at me as if I were some unknown being excavated from the bowels of the earth. I was sipping some brandy-and-water which Burton had handed me, when Aaron Boyce pushed himself in front of me.

"Well, sir," he said, "I am mighty glad you got out of that scrape. I'm bound to say I didn't expect you would. I have been sure all along that it wasn't right to meddle with things that go agin Nature, and I haven't any doubt that you'll see that for yourself and fill up all them tunnels and shafts you've made. The ice that comes on ponds and rivers was good enough for our forefathers, and it ought to be good enough for us. And as for this cold stuff you find in your gravel-pit, I don't believe it's ice at all; and if it is, like as not it's made of some sort of pizen stuff that freezes easier than water. For everybody knows that water don't freeze in a well, and if it don't do that, why should it do it in any kind of a hole in the ground? So perhaps it's just as well that you did git shut up there, sir, and find out for yourself what a dangerous thing it is to fool with Nature and try to git ice from the bottom of the ground instead of the top of the water."

This speech made me angry, for I knew that old Boyce was a man who was always glad to get hold of anything which had gone wrong and to try to make it worse; but I was too weak to answer him.

This, however, would not have been necessary, for Tom Burton turned upon him. "Idiot," said he, "if that is your way of thinking you might as well say that if a well caves in you should never again dig for water, or that nobody should have a cellar under his house for fear that the house should fall into it. There's no more danger of the ice beneath us ever giving way again than there is that this bluff should crumble under our feet. That break in the roof of the ice-tunnel was caused by my digging away the face of the bluff very near that spot. The high temperature of the outer air weakened the ice, and it fell. But down here, under this ground and secure from the influences of the heat of the outer air, the mass of ice is more solid than rock. We will build a brick arch over the place where the accident happened, and then there will not be a safer mine on this continent than this ice-mine will be."

This was a wise and diplomatic speech from Burton, and it proved to be of great service to me; for the men who had been taking out ice had been a good deal frightened by the fall of the tunnel, and when it was proved that what Burton had said in regard to the cause of the weakening of the ice was entirely correct, they became willing to go to work again.

I now began to feel stronger and better, and, rising to my feet, I glanced here and there into the crowd, hoping to catch a sight of Agnes. But I was not very much surprised at not seeing her, because she would naturally shrink from forcing herself into the midst of this motley company; but I felt that I must go and look for her without the loss of a minute, for if she should return to her father's house I might not be able to see her again.

On the outskirts of the crowd I met Susan, who was almost overpowered with joy at seeing me safe again. I shook her by the hand, but, without replying to her warm-hearted protestations of thankfulness and delight, I asked her if she had seen Miss Havelot.

"Miss Agnes!" she exclaimed. "Why, no, sir; I expect she's at home; and if she did come here with the rest of the neighbors I didn't see her; for when I found out what had happened, sir, I was so weak that I sat down in the kitchen all of a lump, and have just had strength enough to come out."

"Oh, I know she was here," I cried; "I am sure of that, and I do hope she's not gone home again."

"Know she was here!" exclaimed Susan. "Why, how on earth could you know that?"

I did not reply that it was not on the earth but under it that I became aware of the fact, but hurried toward the Havelot house, hoping to overtake Agnes if she had gone that way. But I did not see her, and suddenly a startling idea struck me, and I turned and ran home as fast as I could go. When I reached my grounds I went directly to the mouth of the shaft. There was nobody there, for the crowd was collected into a solid mass on the top of the bluff, listening to a lecture from Tom Burton, who deemed it well to promote the growth of interest and healthy opinion in regard to his wonderful discovery and my valuable possession. I hurried down the shaft, and near the end of it, just before it joined the ice-tunnel, I beheld Agnes sitting upon the wooden track. She was not unconscious, for as I approached she slightly turned her head. I sprang toward her; I kneeled beside her; I took her in my arms. "Oh, Agnes, dearest Agnes," I cried, "what is the matter? What has happened to you? Has a piece of ice fallen upon you? Have you slipped and hurt yourself?"

She turned her beautiful eyes up toward me and for a moment did not speak. Then she said: "And they got you out? And you are in your right mind?"

"Right mind!" I exclaimed. "I have never been out of my mind. What are you thinking of?"

"Oh, you must have been," she said; "when you screamed at me in that horrible way. I was so frightened that I fell back, and I must have fainted."

Tremulous as I was with love and anxiety, I could not help laughing. "Oh, my dear Agnes, I did not scream at you. That was a crazed Italian who fell through the hole that they dug." Then I told her what had happened.

She heaved a gentle sigh. "I am so glad to hear that," she said. "There was one thing that I was thinking about just before you came and which gave me a little bit of comfort: the words and yells I heard were dreadfully oniony, and somehow or other I could not connect that sort of thing with you."

It now struck me that during this conversation I had been holding my dear girl in my arms, and she had not shown the slightest sign of resistance or disapprobation. This made my heart beat high. "Oh, Agnes," I said, "I truly believe you love me or you would not have been here, you would not have done for me all that you did. Why did you not answer me when I spoke to you through that wall of ice, through the hole your dear love had made in it? Why, when I was in such a terrible situation, not knowing whether I was to die or live, did you not comfort my heart with one sweet word?"

"Oh, Walter," she answered, "it wasn't at all necessary for you to say all that you did say, for I had suspected it before, and as soon as you began to call me Agnes I knew, of course, how you felt about it. And, besides, it really was necessary that you should move about to keep yourself from freezing. But the great reason for my not encouraging you to go on talking in that way was that I was afraid people might come into the tunnel, and as, of course, you would not know that they were there, you would go on making love to me through my diploma-case, and you know I should have perished with shame if I had had to stand there with that old Mr. Boyce, and I don't know who else, listening to your words, which were very sweet to me, Walter, but which would have sounded awfully funny to them."

When she said that my words had been sweet to her I dropped the consideration of all other subjects.

When, about ten minutes afterward, we came out of the shaft we were met by Susan.

"Bless my soul and body, Mr. Cuthbert!" she exclaimed. "Did you find that young lady down there in the centre of the earth? It seems to me as if everything that you want comes to you out of the ground. But I have been looking for you to tell you that Mr. Havelot has been here after his daughter, and I'm sure if he had known where she was, he would have been scared out of his wits."

"Father here!" exclaimed Agnes. "Where is he now?"

"I think he has gone home, miss. Indeed I'm sure of it; for my daughter Jennie, who was over here the same as all the other people in the county, I truly believe told him — and I was proud she had the spirit to speak up that way to him — that your heart was almost broke when you heard about Mr. Cuthbert being shut up in the ice, and that most likely you was in your own room a-cryin' your eyes out. When he heard that he stood lookin' all around the place, and then he asked me if he might go in the house; and when I told him he was most welcome, he went in. I offered to show him about, which he said was no use, that he had been there often enough; and he went everywhere, I truly believe, except in the garret and the cellar. And after he got through with that he went out to the barn and then walked home."

"I must go to him immediately," said Agnes.

"But not alone," said I. And together we walked through the woods, over the little field and across the Havelot lawn to the house. We were told that the old gentleman was in his library, and together we entered the room.

Mr. Havelot was sitting by a table on which were lying several open volumes of an encyclopedia. When he turned and saw us, he closed his book, pushed back his chair, and took off his spectacles. "Upon my word, sir," he cried; "and so the first thing you do after they pull you out of the earth is to come here and break my commands."

"I came on the invitation of your daughter, sir."

"And what right has she to invite you, I'd like to know?"

"She has every right, for to her I owe my existence."

"What rabid nonsense!" exclaimed the old gentleman. "People don't owe their existence to the silly creatures they fall in love with."

"I assure I am correct, sir." And then I related to him what his daughter had done, and how through her angelic agency my rescuers had found me a living being instead of a frozen corpse.

"Stuff!" said Mr. Havelot. "People can live in a temperature of thirty-two degrees above zero all winter. Out in Minnesota they think that's hot. And you gave him victuals and drink through your diploma-case! Well, miss, I told you that if you tried to roast chestnuts in that diploma-case the bottom would come out."

"But you see, father," said Agnes, earnestly, "the reason I did that was because when I roasted them in anything shallow they popped into the fire, but they could not jump out of the diploma-case."

"Well, something else seems to have jumped out of it," said the old gentleman; "and something with which I am not satisfied. I have been looking over these books, sir, and have read the articles on ice, glaciers, and caves, and I find no record of anything in the whole history of the world which in the least resembles the cock-and-bull story I am told about the butt-end of a glacier which tumbled into a cave in your ground, and has been lying there through all the geological ages, and the eras of formation, and periods of animate existence down to the days of Noah, and Moses, and Methuselah, and Rameses II., and Alexander the Great, and Martin Luther, and John Wesley to this day, for you to dig out and sell to the Williamstown Ice Company."

"But that's what happened, sir," said I.

"And besides, father," added Agnes, "the gold and silver that people take out of mines may have been in the ground as long as that ice has been."

"Bosh!" said Mr. Havelot. "The cases are not at all similar. It is simply impossible that a piece of a glacier should have fallen into a cave and been preserved in that way. The temperature of caves is always above the freezing-point, and that ice would have melted a million years before you were born."

"But, father," said Agnes, "the temperature of caves filled with ice must be very much lower than that of common caves."

"And apart from that," I added, "the ice is still there, sir."

"That doesn't make the slightest difference," he replied. "It's against all reason and common-sense that such a thing could have happened. Even if there ever was a glacier in this part of the country, and if the lower portion of it did stick out over an immense hole in the ground, that protruding end would never have broken off and tumbled in. Glaciers are too thick and massive for that."

"But the glacier is there, sir," said I, "in spite of your own reasoning."

"And then again," continued the old gentleman, "if there had been a cave and a projecting spur the ice would have gradually melted and dripped into the cave, and we would have had a lake and not an ice-mine. It is a perfect absurdity."

"But it's there, notwithstanding," said I.

"And you cannot subvert facts, you know, father," added Agnes.

"Confound facts!" he cried. "I base my arguments on sober, cool-headed reason; and there's nothing that can withstand reason. The thing's impossible and, therefore, it has never happened. I went over to your place, sir, when I heard of the accident, for the misfortunes of my neighbors interest me, no matter what may be my opinion of them, and when I found that you had been extricated from your ridiculous predicament, I went through your house, and I was pleased to find it in as good or better condition than I had known it in the days of your respected father. I was glad to see the improvement in your circumstances; but when I am told, sir, that your apparent prosperity rests upon such an absurdity as a glacier in a gravel-hill, I can but smile with contempt, sir."

I was getting a little tired of this. "But the glacier is there, sir," I said, "and I am taking out ice every day, and have reason to believe that I can continue to take it out for the rest of my life. With such facts as these before me, I am bound to say, sir, that I don't care in the least about reason."

"And I am here, father," said Agnes, coming close to me, "and here I want to continue for the rest of my days."

The old gentleman looked at her. "And, I suppose," he said, "that you, too, don't in the least care about reason?"

"Not a bit," said Agnes.

"Well," said Mr. Havelot, rising, "I have done all I can to make you two listen to reason, and I can do no more. I despair of making sensible human beings of you, and so you might as well go on acting like a couple of ninny-hammers."

"Do ninny-hammers marry and settle on the property adjoining yours, sir?" I asked.

"Yes; I suppose they do," he said. "And when the aboriginal icehouse, or whatever the ridiculous thing is that they have discovered, gives out, I suppose that they can come to a reasonable man and ask him for a little money to buy bread and butter."

Two years have passed, and Agnes and the glacier are still mine; great blocks of ice now flow in almost a continuous stream from the mine to the railroad-station, and in a smaller but quite as continuous stream an income flows in upon Agnes and me; and from one of the experimental excavations made by Tom Burton on the bluff, comes a stream of ice-cold water running in a sparkling brook a-down my dell. On fine mornings before I am up, I am credibly informed that Aaron Boyce may generally be found, in season and out of season, endeavoring to catch the trout with which I am trying to stock that ice-cold stream. The diploma-case, which I caused to be carefully removed from the ice-barrier which had imprisoned me, now hangs in my study and holds our marriage certificate.

Near the line-fence which separates his property from mine, Mr. Havelot has sunk a wide shaft. "If the glacier spur under your land was a quarter of a mile wide," he says to me, "it was probably at least a half a mile long; and if that were the case, the upper end of it extends into my place, and I may be able to strike it." He has a good deal of money, this worthy Mr. Havelot, but he would be very glad to increase his riches, whether they are based upon sound reason or ridiculous facts. As for Agnes and myself, no facts or any reason could make us happier than our ardent love and our frigid fortune.

THE PHILOSOPHY OF RELATIVE EXISTENCES

IN a certain summer, not long gone, my friend Bentley and I found ourselves in a little hamlet which overlooked a placid valley, through which a river gently moved, winding its way through green stretches until it turned the end of a line of low hills and was lost to view. Beyond this river, far away, but visible from the door of the cottage where we dwelt, there lay a city. Through the mists which floated over the valley we could see the outlines of steeples and tall roofs; and buildings of a character which indicated thrift and business stretched themselves down to the opposite edge of the river. The more distant parts of the city, evidently a small one, lost themselves in the hazy summer atmosphere.

Bentley was young, fair-haired, and a poet; I was a philosopher, or trying to be one. We were good friends, and had come down into this peaceful region to work together. Although we had fled from the bustle and distractions of the town, the appearance in this rural region of a city, which, so far as we could observe, exerted no influence on the quiet character of the valley in which it lay, aroused our interest. No craft plied up and down the river; there were no bridges from shore to shore; there were none of those scattered and half-squalid habitations which generally are found on the outskirts of a city; there came to us no distant sound of bells; and not the smallest wreath of smoke rose from any of the buildings.

In answer to our inquiries our landlord told us that the city over the river had been built by one man, who was a visionary, and who had a great deal more money than common sense. "It is not as big a town as you would think, sirs," he said, "because the general mistiness of things in this valley makes them look larger than they are. Those hills, for instance, when you get to them are not as high as they look to be from here. But the town is big enough, and a good deal too big; for it ruined its builder and owner, who when he came to die had not money enough left to put up a decent tombstone at the head of his grave. He had a queer idea that he would like to have his town all finished before anybody lived in it, and so he kept on working and spending money year after year and year after year until the city was done and he had not a cent left. During all the time that the place was building hundreds of people came to him to buy houses or to hire them, but he would not listen to anything of the kind. No one must live in his town until it was all done. Even his workmen were obliged to go away at night to lodge. It is a town, sirs, I am told, in which nobody has slept for even a night. There are streets there, and places of business, and churches, and public halls, and everything that a town full of inhabitants could need; but it is all empty and deserted, and has been so as far back as I can remember, and I came to this region when I was a little boy."

"And is there no one to guard the place?" we asked; "no one to protect it from wandering vagrants who might choose to take possession of the buildings?"

"There are not many vagrants in this part of the country," he said; "and if there were, they would not go over to that city. It is haunted."

"By what?" we asked.

"Well, sirs, I scarcely can tell you; queer beings that are not flesh and blood, and that is all I know about it. A good many people living hereabouts have visited that place once in their lives, but I know of no one who has gone there a second time."

"And travellers," I said; "are they not excited by curiosity to explore that strange uninhabited city?"

"Oh, yes," our host replied; "almost all visitors to the valley go over to that queer city — generally in small parties, for it is not a place in which one wishes to walk about alone. Sometimes they see things, and sometimes they don't. But I never knew any man or woman to show a fancy for living there, although it is a very good town."

This was said at supper-time, and, as it was the period of full moon, Bentley and I decided that we would visit the haunted city that evening. Our host endeavored to dissuade us, saying that no one ever went over there at night; but as we were not to be deterred, he told us where we would find his small boat tied to a stake on the river-bank. We soon crossed the river, and landed at a broad, but low, stone pier, at the land end of which a line of tall grasses waved in the gentle night wind as if they were sentinels warning us from entering the silent city. We pushed through these, and walked up a street fairly wide, and so well paved that we noticed none of the weeds and other growths which generally denote desertion or little use. By the bright light of the moon we could see that the architecture was simple, and of a character highly gratifying to the eye. All the buildings were of stone and of good size. We were greatly excited and interested, and proposed to continue our walks until the moon should set, and to return on the following morning — "to live here, perhaps," said Bentley. "What could be so romantic and yet so real? What could conduce better to the marriage of verse and philosophy?" But as he said this we saw around the corner of a cross-street some forms as of people hurrying away.

"The spectres," said my companion, laying his hand on my arm.

"Vagrants, more likely," I answered, "who have taken advantage of the superstition of the region to appropriate this comfort and beauty to themselves."

"If that be so," said Bentley, "we must have a care for our lives."

We proceeded cautiously, and soon saw other forms fleeing before us and disappearing, as we supposed, around corners and into houses. And now suddenly finding ourselves upon the edge of a wide, open public square, we saw in the dim light — for a tall steeple obscured the moon — the forms of vehicles, horses, and men moving here and there. But before, in our astonishment, we could say a word one to the other, the moon moved past the steeple, and in its bright light we could see none of the signs of life and traffic which had just astonished us.

Timidly, with hearts beating fast, but with not one thought of turning back, nor any fear of vagrants,—for we were now sure that what we had seen was not flesh and blood, and therefore harmless,—we crossed the open space and entered a street down which the moon shone clearly. Here and there we saw dim figures, which quickly disappeared; but, approaching a low stone balcony in front of one of the houses, we were surprised to see, sitting thereon and leaning over a book which lay open upon the top of the carved parapet, the figure of a woman who did not appear to notice us.

"That is a real person," whispered Bentley, "and she does not see us."

"No," I replied; "it is like the others. Let us go near it."

We drew near to the balcony and stood before it. At this the figure raised its head and looked at us. It was beautiful, it was young; but its substance seemed to be of an ethereal quality which we had never seen or known of. With its full, soft eyes fixed upon us, it spoke:—

"Why are you here?" it asked. "I have said to myself that the next time I saw any of you I would ask you why you come to trouble us. Cannot you live content in your own realms and spheres, knowing, as you must know, how timid we are, and how you frighten us and make us unhappy? In all this city there is, I believe, not one of us except myself who does not flee and hide from you whenever you cruelly come here. Even I would do that, had not I declared to myself that I would see you and speak to you, and endeavor to prevail upon you to leave us in peace."

The clear, frank tones of the speaker gave me courage. "We are two men," I answered, "strangers in this region, and living for the time in the beautiful country on the other side of the river. Having heard of this quiet city, we have come to see it for ourselves. We had supposed it to be uninhabited, but now that we find that this is not the case, we would assure you from our hearts that we do not wish to disturb or annoy any one who lives here. We simply came as honest travellers to view the city."

The figure now seated herself again, and as her countenance was nearer to us, we could see that it was filled with pensive thought. For a moment she looked at us without speaking. "Men!" she said. "And so I have been right. For a long time I have believed that the beings who sometimes come here, filling us with dread and awe, are men."

"And you," I exclaimed — "who are you, and who are these forms that we have seen, these strange inhabitants of this city?"

She gently smiled as she answered: "We are the ghosts of the future. We are the people who are to live in this city generations hence. But all of us do not know that, principally because we do not think about it and study about it enough to know it. And it is generally believed that the men and women who sometimes come here are ghosts who haunt the place."

"And that is why you are terrified and flee from us?" I exclaimed. "You think we are ghosts from another world?"

"Yes," she replied; "that is what is thought, and what I used to think."

"And you," I asked, "are spirits of human beings yet to be?"

"Yes," she answered; "but not for a long time. Generations of men, I know not how many, must pass away before we are men and women."

"Heavens!" exclaimed Bentley, clasping his hands and raising his eyes to the sky, "I shall be a spirit before you are a woman."

"Perhaps," she said again, with a sweet smile upon her face, "you may live to be very, very old."

But Bentley shook his head. This did not console him. For some minutes I stood in contemplation, gazing upon the stone pavement beneath my feet. "And this," I ejaculated, "is a city inhabited by the ghosts of the future, who believe men and women to be phantoms and spectres?"

She bowed her head.

"But how is it," I asked, "that you discovered that you are spirits and we mortal men?"

"There are so few of us who think of such things," she answered, "so few who study, ponder, and reflect. I am fond of study, and I love philosophy; and from the reading of many books I have learned much. From the book which I have here I have learned most; and from its teachings I have gradually come to the belief, which you tell me is the true one, that we are spirits and you men."

"And what book is that?" I asked.

"It is 'The Philosophy of Relative Existences,' by Rupert Vance."

"Ye gods!" I exclaimed, springing upon the balcony, "that is my book, and I am Rupert Vance." I stepped toward the volume to seize it, but she raised her hand.

"You cannot touch it," she said. "It is the ghost of a book. And did you write it?"

"Write it? No," I said; "I am writing it. It is not yet finished."

"But here it is," she said, turning over the last pages. "As a spirit book it is finished. It is very successful; it is held in high estimation by intelligent thinkers; it is a standard work."

I stood trembling with emotion. "High estimation!" I said. "A standard work!"

"Oh, yes," she replied with animation; "and it well deserves its great success, especially in its conclusion. I have read it twice."

"But let me see these concluding pages," I exclaimed. "Let me look upon what I am to write."

She smiled, and shook her head, and closed the book. "I would like to do that," she said, "but if you are really a man you must not know what you are going to do."

"Oh, tell me, tell me," cried Bentley from below, "do you know a book called 'Stellar Studies,' by Arthur Bentley? It is a book of poems."

The figure gazed at him. "No," it said presently; "I never heard of it."

I stood trembling. Had the youthful figure before

me been flesh and blood, had the book been a real one, I would have torn it from her.

"O wise and lovely being!" I exclaimed, falling on my knees before her, "be also benign and generous. Let me but see the last page of my book. If I have been of benefit to your world; more than all, if I have been of benefit to you, let me see, I implore you — let me see how it is that I have done it."

She rose with the book in her hand. "You have only to wait until you have done it," she said, "and then you will know all that you could see here." I started to my feet, and stood alone upon the balcony.

"I am sorry," said Bentley, as we walked toward the pier where we had left our boat, "that we talked only to that ghost girl, and that the other spirits were all afraid of us. Persons whose souls are choked up with philosophy are not apt to care much for poetry; and even if my book is to be widely known, it is easy to see that she may not have heard of it."

I walked triumphant. The moon, almost touching the horizon, beamed like red gold. "My dear friend," said I, "I have always told you that you should put more philosophy into your poetry. That would make it live."

"And I have always told you," said he, "that you should not put so much poetry into your philosophy. It misleads people."

"It didn't mislead that ghost girl," said I.

"How do you know?" said Bentley. "Perhaps she is wrong, and the other inhabitants of the city are right, and we may be the ghosts after all. Such things, you know, are only relative. Anyway," he continued, after a little pause, "I wish I knew that those ghosts were now reading the poem which I am going to begin to-morrow."

THE KNIFE THAT KILLED PO HANCY

PO HANCY was the chief of a band of Dacoit robbers, those outlaws who for years have ravaged portions of British Burmah, killing, stealing, and burning, and regarding not whether the sufferers were their own people or white-skinned foreigners. Prominent among these midnight assassins and robbers was Po Hancy; but he came to his just reward at last, being trapped and killed by two native spies, and the knife by which his head was severed from his body lay on my library table. It had been sent to me by a missionary friend to whom it had been brought as a trophy of the superior valor of the loyal and somewhat civilized natives over that of the outlaws of the jungle. It was a rude weapon, with a heavy blade nearly nine inches long, enclosed in a wooden sheath, and with a beautifully polished handle of bone-like wood. On the point of the blade and on its sides were great blotches of rust, caused by the blood of Po Hancy.

This formidable weapon with its history was very interesting to me; I could sympathize with the joyful satisfaction with which the little band of missionaries had looked upon the knife as a blessed sleep-giver, an assurance that they need no longer lie awake on account of rumors of the approach of that bloodthirsty and unconvertible heathen and his band.

More than that, it had another interest for me; it made me think of the man who had come to his death by it. The idea struck me that Po Hancy and I were as different from each other as two human beings could possibly be. To arrange our differences in a tabulated statement would be a work of a good deal of time and very little value, but there was one dissimilarity between us that particularly impressed itself upon me: I had heard a good deal of this tiger-like Dacoit crawling through the jungles for ten, fifteen, or twenty miles, leaping down rocks with foothold as silent and certain as that of a cat, and bounding upon his victims with a strength and swiftness of an untiring beast of prey.

How different was I — a languid, soft-fleshed, almost middle-aged lawyer, tired out by sedentary work, by night and by day, to whom a walk of half a mile was weariness, and a climb to my office on the fifth floor of a lofty building was a backache. As a young man I had been somewhat athletic, but years of too much work of one kind, and too little of another, had made activity a memory, and wholesome exercise a discomfort. Po Hancy was a specimen of perfect animal life, and of the most imperfect life of the mind and soul. My body resembled his mind and soul; of my mind and soul I will say nothing, being of a modest disposition.

Po Hancy was gone, utterly departed and annihilated, with the exception of the atoms of dried blood which might yet remain in the blotches of rust upon this ugly knife-blade. Strangely enough, it was possible that something which helped to make up that fierce Dacoit, some portions, minute though they might be, of his very self, might lie here before me, in my library, by my prayer-book, and a recent letter from my mother, in a home of high civilization, on the other side of the world from the Burmese jungle.

As I sat thinking of these things I took out my pocket-knife, and began to scratch the spots of rust upon the blade, and succeeded in detaching a little of the fine dust from the iron, oxidized by means of Po Hancy's life currents. There was so little of it, that I had to moisten the end of my knife-blade in order to take it up, and carefully look at it. Of course to the eye it was like any other iron rust, but to my mind it was far different. If there really were still atoms of blood in it, it was all, or nearly all, that remained above earth of the famous Po Hancy.

Involuntarily I balanced my penknife on my finger, as if to weigh this infinitesimal remnant of savage mortality, when suddenly the knife slipped, and in endeavoring to catch it, the point ran into the thumb of my left hand, inflicting a slight wound. For a moment I was frightened. Here was an example of the folly of playing with edged tools, especially those that had belonged to savage heathens. This knife of the slayer of the Dacoit might have been poisoned, and here I had wounded myself with the point of my own knife, to which adhered the dust I had scraped from it. It was horrible to think that in a few hours I might perish by the same knife that slew that ferocious murderer!

After a time, however, I calmed myself, for I had never heard that the Burmese used poisoned weapons, and when several days had passed without my having felt any evil effects from the wound, which soon healed, I felt perfectly safe. In fact, instead of there being any injurious result from the cut (or the not inconsiderable nervous shock consequent upon it), I found myself in rather better health than usual, and one afternoon I walked across the Common, through the Public Garden, and four or five blocks beyond, to my home, and did not feel the least fatigue. I had not had an experience of this kind for two or three years.

During the next few weeks, many of my friends remarked that my health was certainly improving, and there could be no doubt that they were correct. I began to take walks that were moderately long. I played billiards, that used to tire me so much that I seldom played a whole game. And what surprised everybody, and myself quite as much, I joined an athletic club. This numbered among its members a dozen or more of my friends, nearly all of whom, at one time or another, had pressed me to join the club, assuring me that it was the best thing I could do if I wished to regain my old strength and activity, but I had always refused. The very idea of gymnastic exercise was disagreeable to me, and I was annoyed at their persistence in advising it.

Now they were astonished at my change of opinion, and some of them were inclined to ridicule me, suggesting some very easy and mild methods of exercise suitable for a small boy beginner. But they stopped that sort of chaff, when I raised a vaulting-bar several inches higher than the last performer had left it, and then went over it without touching; and when, seizing a trapeze bar, I drew up my body and threw myself around it with the ease of a circus man, some of them remembered that I used to do that sort of thing, but that I could return to it now, after all these years of desk work, amazed them.

I kept up my gymnastic exercises nearly every day, and as the club was to give a public exhibition early in the autumn, I felt inclined to take part in it. All my love for athletic sport had returned. But in spite of my undoubted activity, there were a good many men in the club who were greatly my superiors in athletic feats, and there was no reason to suppose that I would achieve any especial distinction in the public games. The conviction of this somewhat dampened my desire to become a contestant on so important an occasion, and I sat down one evening to consider the matter. "In the first place," I said to myself, "how did I regain all my old strength and activity? I have not altered my method of living, my diet is the same, I have had no change of air." At this moment my eye fell on the knife that killed Po Hancy, which still lay upon my table. "By George!" I exclaimed, springing to my feet, "could it have been that?"

My face flushed and my whole form glowed as I remembered how I had fancied I had poisoned myself by introducing into my veins the stuff I had scraped from the Burmese knife. And now, could it be? Was it by any means possible that I had accidentally inoculated myself with some of the blood of Po

Hancy, and in so doing had introduced into my system some of his savage vigor and agility!

The more I thought of this, the more strongly I became convinced that it was so. I am a scientist in an amateur way, and I take a great interest in experiments such as those performed by Brown-Sequard and Dr. Koch. If certain physical attributes of one class of living beings could be communicated to another by inoculation, or hypodermic injection, why should not another physical attribute be transmitted in the same way? I could see no reason why this should not be so, and in fact, I believed myself a proof that the thing could be done.

Now, if I possessed some of the high physical qualities of the defunct Po Hancy, why should I not possess them to a greater degree? What he had in perfection was what I lacked. If I could get what he no longer needed, and what, indeed, I would gladly have deprived him of, whether I had been able to get it or not, why should I not have it? There was really nothing to object to in this proposition, and I determined to make an experiment.

Rubbing some glycerine over the blood spots upon the Dacoit knife, I scraped vigorously until I accumulated a little mass of the gummy substance. Then baring my left arm, and excoriating a little spot on it, as if I were about to vaccinate myself, I rubbed in the compound. "Now," said I, wrapping a handkerchief around my arm, "we shall see what we shall see."

The next morning, our waitress, who was just entering the breakfast room, saw what she did see. She saw me come in at another door, look at the table set ready for the family breakfast, with a large bouquet, a foot and a half high, in the centre of the table, run a few steps, and then bound entirely over said table, bouquet and all, and come down upon the other side with an elastic thud, as if I had been made of India rubber. She screamed, and although I had not touched anything, stood expecting a crash.

"Merciful me, sir!" she exclaimed, when she found nothing was about to happen; "I never did see anybody so supple."

When my two sisters came down,—with me they made up the family, for my mother was in Europe,—I had to tell them about this jump, for I did not want the girl to do it.

"I have noticed, Harry," said Amelia, "that you have changed very much of late. You are as springy as a Jack-in-the-Box, and you used to be so poky and stiff. I think you ought not to do that sort of thing in the house. Suppose you had swept everything off this table, what a lot of damage you would have done. And I have had to have the stair-carpet stretched and replaced because you will persist in going up three steps at a time, and getting it all out of shape."

"I am very glad that Harry is feeling so strong and well," said Jenny; "and I am going to teach him to play tennis."

I laughed internally as I thought of a man with my nimble power playing a baby game like tennis.

The inoculation with the blood of Po Hancy was undoubtedly a success. I could feel strength and vigor bounding through my veins; without hesitation

I announced myself as a candidate for athletic honors in the approaching games.

I will not here relate the feats I performed on the great field of our club. In contests of hurling, lifting, and all that, I took no part; but in running, jumping, vaulting, bounding, I excelled all competitors and broke several records. Had Po Hancy been in my place, he might have done better, but without the influence of Po Hancy's wild blood no one on the grounds could have done as well. This is what I said to myself as the crowd roared out its applause, and my friends gathered around me to shake my hand.

Not only was my whole habit of life changed, but the changes went on. I was not content to be able to bound like a tiger and run like a deer, but I wanted to do these things. Several times when coming home from my office in the evening, I was stopped by policemen who wanted to know what I was running away from. I had some difficulty in persuading them that I ran purely from a love of exercise, and they advised against such speed in the public streets. Late at night I used to have grand runs in the Common, but this did not suit me very well. There were sometimes observers, and the place was too open. I liked better the Public Gardens, which afterward became my nightly exercise ground.

With a pair of soft tennis-shoes on my feet it was my delight to steal swiftly around masses of shrubbery, dart up avenues, slip before the eyes of astonished policemen, and vanish into the shade, to bound into the branches of some heavily foliaged tree, and watch the guardian of the peace stalking below me, and then when he had passed, to drop noiselessly down to track him over the whole of his beat, without his suspecting that my soft-falling footsteps followed his.

I did not pay much attention to my business, as had been my custom, and I indulged in exercise and long walks, even in the daytime, when I should have been at my office. I felt a great desire to hunt — I do not mean to follow the hounds in their courses about the Boston suburbs, but to tramp through the wild woods and kill things with a rifle. As there was little scope for this sort of sport in the coast country of Massachusetts, I wanted to take a trip to the lower part of Florida, for it was too late in the season to go far West. In the forests down there I was sure I could still find wild game, and if a wandering Seminole Indian happened to interfere with me, or a reckless alligator-hunter picked a quarrel with me, I felt that I would be very well able to take care of myself.

My law partners, however, objected very strongly to my leaving town in the midst of our busiest season, and I was obliged to postpone my contemplated trip. One of the members of our firm jocosely remarked to me that so far as business was concerned I was a better man when I was not so well. And my sisters, who used to object to walking with me because I was so much given to going slowly, and stopping often, now declined to accompany me because I strode so rapidly that it tired them to keep up with me. In fact, in the whole of Boston, I did not know any one who shared my fancies for what might be called super-exercise, and I was obliged to be content with my own company in my morning bounces and my evening spins.

But it must not be supposed that I lost at this time my desire for companionship; in truth, a novel desire of that sort sprang up within me. A distant relative of my mother, who had always been accustomed to spend some weeks with us in the autumn, now came to make her annual visit. This was a lady of thirty or thereabouts, by the name of Susan Mooney. She was the kindest, gentlest, quietest, softest woman in the world. Her disposition was so tender that if one spoke to her of trouble or pain, the tears would almost always come into her eyes.

My sisters were sorry that Susan had made her visit this year during the absence of our mother; for although they liked her and loved her, they did not find her a congenial companion. They were lively girls, fond of society, while she was the quietest of the quiet, and fond of home. Consequently, they were well pleased when they found that I seemed to fancy Susan's company, for that relieved them of the burden. But after a week or two their feelings changed, and they told me they thought I was giving entirely too much of my time to Susan. My family had come to look upon me as a bachelor who would never think of marrying, and it would have surprised them to see me paying marked attention to any lady. But when my sisters saw me paying attention, so very marked indeed, to Susan Mooney, they were not only surprised, but offended.

"If you are going to marry anybody," said Amelia, "do take some one who is suitable for you. Mother is very fond of Susan, and we like her, but she would never do for a wife for you. She is no better than a bag of milk."

I looked at them and smiled. It was true that I had taken Susan to the theatre or concerts, evening after evening, although I had been in the habit of declining to go to such places with my sisters; that I made her take long walks with me; that I spent hours with her when I should have been in my office; and that lately she had been known to flush a little when I came into the room where she was.

"Susan Mooney," I said, "is exactly the kind of girl — or lady — that I like. She is so gentle, so docile, so submissive, that —"

"Submissive!" snapped Jenny; "I should think so. She has not the least bit of will of her own. You would become a perfect tyrant with a wife like that. I believe she would grow to tremble when she heard your footstep."

"I do not say," I answered, "that I am going to marry Susan, nor that I am going to marry anybody; but if I ever do take a wife, I want one who will tremble when she hears my footstep."

They both laughed. "For a mild-mannered man," cried Amelia, "you talk bigger than any one I ever heard. The idea that any one could ever tremble at your footstep is ridiculous."

I made no answer. It was well that they could not analyze the blood that now ran in my veins. To me Susan Mooney was attractive to a degree that no other woman had been. I would not cease my attentions to her, but, perhaps, since my sisters seemed so observant, I would be more wary about them.

I had used to be somewhat of a submissive person myself, but I was such no longer. I did not always state my determination to do things against the opinions and wishes of others, but the determination was never altered. I grew to like to put myself in opposition, especially if the other party did not know how I stood. This I flattered myself might be a good thing for a lawyer, but it was very different from my old methods of thought and action. I also felt occasional desires to put myself in physical opposition to some one. I did not feel quarrelsome, but if I had seen a reasonable opportunity of obtruding my physical superiority on a fellow-being, I should have been glad to avail myself of it. Civilized society does not offer chances of this sort, sufficiently often, to satisfy Po Hancyish cravings.

One evening as I was sitting in my library and study on the third floor, I heard a slight noise downstairs as if from the opening of a door. I knew that the rest of the family had all retired, and I naturally thought that a burglar was trying to enter the house. The moment this idea came into my mind, my whole body thrilled with a warm ecstasy. I slipped off my shoes, and stole to the top of the stairs and listened — I heard the noise again! Darting back into my room, I buttoned my dark coat tight around my neck to conceal my white collar, and then seizing the knife that killed Po Hancy, I silently glided down the stairway. My eyes must have glistened with the expectant joy of meeting a burglar. What transporting delight it would be to steal upon the rascal and slay him with one blow. It is so seldom that one gets an opportunity to legitimately slay a rascal, or indeed any one. I do not say that I would have decoyed a burglar into the house for the purpose of slaying him, but if one were really here of his own accord, how gladly would I exercise my legal rights.

Down the stairs I went, bending low, with eyes peering into the dark, with ears stretched to catch the slightest sound, and with the knife that killed Po Hancy half raised in my right hand. I went through all the rooms on the first floor, I descended into the cellar, feeling my way about in the darkness, and stopping at intervals to listen. I even penetrated to the back of the coal-bin, and I remember thinking with pride how I stepped so carefully as to scarcely disturb the coals that were piled about me.

Suddenly I heard the same noise that I had noticed before. It was above me, and with a quick and silent bound I was at the top of the cellar stairs. Here I found what had made the noise; it was a door at this spot which had been left open. I noticed that it was not fastened when I came down, but thought nothing of it. A ventilating window was near by, and when a puff of wind came into this window the door was opened a little way, and then slowly swung back of its own inclination.

When I discovered the facts of the case, I could almost have cried. I felt that I had sustained a cruel disappointment. Chagrined and depressed, I walked slowly into the dining-room and sat down, debating with myself whether or not I would care to put on my hat and take a long night run. While sitting thus, I heard some one coming down the stairs with slow and deliberate footsteps. I knew those footsteps; they were those of Mary Carpenter, our good old housekeeper. Ashamed that she should find me sitting in the dark, I got up and began to look for matches, but before I found them, she entered, carrying a lighted candle.

"Mercy on me, Mr. Harry!" she exclaimed. "What on earth are you doing here in the dark? I just remembered that I did not fasten the top cellar door, and I came down to do it. Are you sick?"

"No," I answered; "I am hungry, and I came down to get some pie. I was just going to strike a light."

"Well, well!" exclaimed the good Mary; "that is just like you, Mr. Harry. When you were a boy, and even a young man, you were always wanting to eat pie at night, and there were some that said that you would have had better health if you had not done so much of it. But for my part, I can't see any harm in eating good wholesome pie, when a body feels hungry for it. I have not heard you say you wanted some pie for a long while, and it seems like good old times to give you some after everybody else is in bed. Now, it is lucky that I made to-day, with my own hands, the first pumpkin pies of the season. I'll get one and cut you a piece. Goodness gracious, Mr. Harry! You didn't mean to cut one of my pies with that horrible knife, did you? If you did, I am truly glad that I came down in time to stop you. A heathen knife in a Christian pie is something I never heard of yet, and I hope never to. It would poison it."

In a few minutes the good Mary placed before me a noble specimen of her pastry-cooking.

"There," said she, "is a pumpkin pie fit for a king, only kings never get them; and I suppose they would call it a pudding in England, if they had it at all. It's a good inch and a half thick, the way you always liked them, and I am sure a piece of it will not hurt you."

She cut a generous segment of the pie and gave it to me on a plate. She was delighted to see with what pleasure I ate it, and when I asked for another piece she was surprised, but gave it to me. When I asked for a third piece, she demurred a little, but in spite of her really earnest protestations, I helped myself to more, and eventually finished the whole pie, which was of a size sufficient for an ordinary family.

"Well, well!" said Mary, as she took away my plate and the empty pie-dish; "this beats anything you ever did when you were a boy. I only hope that you won't feel badly in the night; but if you do, come to my door and knock. It won't take me a minute to mix some peppermint for you, or give you anything else you need."

I did not wonder that the good Mary was astonished at the midnight appetite of a Po Hancy. I began to fear, however, that I had been imprudent in letting this appetite run away with me, and felt very glad that there was some one in the house who knew what to do for victims of unreasonable voracity. However, there was no occasion for her services, for I went to bed and slept the sleep of an infant. In the morning when I awoke, fresh and clear-headed, with a wholesome appetite for my breakfast, I felt what it was to possess the digestion of a Dacoit.

The wonderful physical powers with which I felt myself endowed were sources of the greatest satisfaction to me, but they began to have their drawbacks, and after a time they caused me great mental uneasiness. Because I knew myself perfectly able to do certain things which I ought not to do, I wished to do them. For instance, there was a stout man of German Jewish aspect, who, before my Po Hancy days, had been in the habit of going home from his business about the same time that I did, and frequently took the street car in which I was riding. This man, if it were possible, always seated himself next to me, thinking, I imagined, that as I was rather a slender man, he would have a better chance of crowding me, and getting more than his share of room in case the car became full. And when this opportunity was afforded him, he always availed himself of it to the utmost. I sometimes remonstrated with him, and sometimes tried to crowd him a little; but neither course was of any service, and it not unfrequently happened that I got up and stood on the platform to avoid this unsavory persecutor.

As I now thought of this man, my blood boiled within me. I did not, at this time, ride in street cars, for I felt no need of them, but I felt greatly tempted to get into one at the hour I usually left my office, in the hope that the stout man would enter and sit beside me. If this should happen, and he should dare to push or elbow me, I would spring upon him and hurl him out of the door of the car, no matter how rapidly it might be moving. I ground my teeth in savage anticipation of the joy I would take in thus avenging myself for all his former insults. But my common sense and my familiarity with the common law showed me that this would be a very foolish thing to do, certain to bring me into trouble, and even ridicule, which would be worse. My uncivilized instincts were so strong that frequently I was obliged, figuratively, to put my hand upon my own shoulder to prevent myself from entering a car in which there was a chance of encountering the stout German.

There were other novel and perhaps aboriginal cravings which came upon me at this time. One of these was an abnormal longing to possess desirable objects. For instance, in a jeweller's window, which I frequently passed, there was a handsome brooch which attracted my favorable attention. It was composed of a large stone of the moonstone order, artistically surrounded by brilliants. It struck me that this would be a most appropriate ornament for the gentle Susan. Several times I stood looking at it and planning how I might get it for her without resort to the usual methods of exchange. A strong tap on the window pane, a quick snatch, and then a series of dartings and doublings, along a route which I had marked out in my mind, — around a corner, up an alley, over the fences of two back yards that I had noted, into a small street, where I would change my soft light-colored felt hat for a dark travelling-cap which I would have in my pocket. Then a rush into a crowded thoroughfare, and a leisurely walk home. But this scheme did not altogether please me; I would have better liked, in the dark hours of the morning, to climb a tree which stood before the jeweller's shop, to go out on a limb until it bent down to the level of the transom window over the top of the door, to open this, slip in, pocket the brooch, climb up to the transom, listen, drop outside, and noiselessly glide away.

I had entirely too many fancies of this kind, and when away from my temptations, my mind was seriously troubled by the thoughts of the dangers to which I was exposed; this robber blood was making a different man of me, a man who ran the risk of ending his life in a prison. I used to ponder for hours upon my alarming condition. Sometimes I thought of myself as another Mr. Hyde; but alas! my case was worse than that. I was not sometimes good and sometimes bad; I was under an influence which was steadfast and of increasing power, the effects of which, my reason told me, must be permanent. When a Christian gentleman puts Dacoit blood into his veins, there is no way of his getting it out again, except by letting out all of his blood,—a remedy I did not fancy. How earnestly I wished Po Hancy had been converted before he had been killed.

But had the robber chief repented and lived a proper life, he would not have been killed, and I would have had no knife with his blood on it, and my present physical perfection would never have come to me. When I looked upon the matter in this light, I asked myself whether I would have been satisfied had it been so, and I could not bring myself to answer Yes. After all, it was my vanity that had brought this terrible peril upon me. Had I been contented with the little prick my knife had given me, I might have been no more than the active, healthy gentleman

I had always wished to be. But that foolish desire to shine in the athletic games had not only given me an excess of strength, but also the impulses of a jungle sneak.

When troubled thus, my greatest relief was the society of Susan Mooney. The flow of her gentle soul was so unrippled that it seldom failed to soothe me. Feeling the great good she was to me, I now made up my mind to marry her, and it delighted me to think that in so doing I would not be troubled by the ordinary antecedents of matrimony. I would simply inform her that she was to be my wife, then all she would have to do was to set herself to the task of getting ready for the ceremony. But I could not always avail myself of the soothings of Susan, and the agitation of my mind became more harassing and frequent.

Early one evening I was sitting alone in my study, torn by a desire to take a long walk in the suburbs, and restrained by a fear that if I did so I should be induced to forget that I was not a prowling Dacoit. Suddenly I heard a cry below stairs; it was the voice of my dear Susan, in terror and pain. In ten seconds I had bounded down to the drawing-room, where, between my two sisters, I found the fair Susan almost fainting with one of her white hands reddened with her blood, and in her lap the knife that killed Po Hancy. The situation was quickly explained; that afternoon Jenny had brought down the knife to show a visitor interested in such things, and now Susan had been playing with it and had cut her finger!

The wound was not a serious one, and the sufferer was soon cared for and conducted to her room. I took the knife upstairs, determined to lock it up securely. But as I was about to replace it in its sheath I noticed that the blade was discolored in several places with fresh blood — the blood of Susan, still moist.

I sat for some ten minutes, earnestly gazing upon the knife-blade. What a contrast — the blood of Po Hancy, the blood of Susan Mooney. As I pondered, a thought, seemingly filled with the light of a coming salvation, dawned upon me. I bared my right arm, and with my penknife scratched the skin for a space of over an inch in diameter. On this I rubbed the moist blood of Susan, as much of it as I could get from the great knife-blade, and which exceeded in quantity that which I had obtained from the rust spots. I trembled when this deed was finished; I did not dare to think what might happen, but I hoped.

The next day my right arm was very sore, and I could not write. I felt assured that no one with Dacoit blood in his veins should be allowed to perform an operation of the nature of vaccination. As my disability, the cause of which I did not explain to any one, gave a reason for a little vacation, I went off to the Berkshire Hills. The gay season of Stockbridge and Lenox had not yet come to an end, and the life there interested me very much. It was a pleasant change; for years I had mingled very little in fashionable society. I met a good many friends and acquaintances, all glad to have me with them, but surprised as well as pleased at my willingness to enter into all the festive doings of the region. In fact, I agreed to whatever was proposed to me, except when two of my fellow-members of the athletic club asked me to join them in a long tramp. This I declined, mainly for the reason that they had planned to start very early in the morning before sunrise, and I would not give up the delightful and tranquillizing hours of sleep which immediately precede a late breakfast.

At the close of the day after my return I rode home from my office in a street car. At the corner where I had been in the habit of expecting him, the stout German got in. There was an empty place next to me, large enough for an ordinary person, but not large enough for him. He came directly toward me and endeavored to squeeze himself into the vacancy. As he did so, I moved as far as possible away from him, in order to give him the room he desired.

That evening my sister Amelia took me aside. "Harry," said she, "I have something very serious to say to you. Susan has had a letter from mother begging her to stay here until her return. Now, this will keep her with us a month longer at least, and I think this is a very deplorable thing."

"Why so?" I asked.

"Because it will give you an opportunity to carry on your absurd courtship of her, and that cannot fail to end in your marrying her, and I should like to know, Harry, what could be more deplorable than that? In fact, Jenny and I have made up our minds that we will not stand it. Mother may consent to live in the house with that simple Susan as your wife, but we never will."

"My dear sister," said I, "you and Jenny need not trouble yourselves on that subject. I do not in the least desire to marry Susan Mooney. She is a good woman, very good, but she is not the sort of person I would want for a wife. I should think you could see that for yourselves. The life of a hard-working man like myself is monotonous enough without Susan. But now that you have spoken of marriage, I will say that I met two ladies, one in Stockbridge and the other at Lenox, either of which would make me a good wife. I rather prefer the Lenox girl, Miss Camilla Sunderland. Do you know her?"

"Camilla Sunderland!" exclaimed my sister. "She is a leading belle, a dazzling star of the season. She goes everywhere, does everything, drives four-in-hand, plays tennis matches, is devoted to balls, theatre parties — why, my dear Harry, I should think you could not exist with a wife like that."

"Miss Sunderland," said I, leaning back in a soft armchair, "would be just the wife I dream of. I am sure I prefer her to the lady at Stockbridge. I am not disposed, as you know, to take part, to any great extent, in the exciting life of the fashionable world, but I should wish to feel that through my wife I had a part in it."

"Well!" exclaimed Amelia, "you may never get Camilla Sunderland, but I am truly glad that you have given up all thoughts of Susan. But, Harry, a very great change must have come over you; it was not long ago that you told me you wanted a wife who would tremble at your tread."

I made a gesture of languid disapprobation. "My dear girl," said I, "I should despise a woman who would tremble at my tread."

I have not yet married Miss Sunderland, partly because it is difficult for a man of my quiet and slow turn of mind to follow and find her in the mazes and intricacies of the fashionable life in which she exists, and partly because my sisters have succeeded in making me doubt her acceptance of my addresses in case I should get an opportunity of offering them to her. But I want her, and until she is married to somebody else, I shall continue to hope.

As for the knife that killed Po Hancy, I threw it into the Charles River. It was a dangerous knife.

THE CHRISTMAS SHADRACH

WHENEVER I make a Christmas present I like it to mean something; not necessarily my sentiments toward the person to whom I give it, but sometimes an expression of what I should like that person to do or to be. In the early part of a certain winter not very long ago I found myself in a position of perplexity and anxious concern regarding a Christmas present which I wished to make.

The state of the case was this. There was a young lady, the daughter of a neighbor and old friend of my father, who had been gradually assuming relations toward me which were not only unsatisfactory to me, but were becoming more and more so. Her name was Mildred Bronce. She was between twenty and twenty-five years of age, and as fine a woman in every way as one would be likely to meet in a lifetime. She was handsome, of a tender and generous disposition, a fine intelligence, and a thoroughly well-stocked mind. We had known each other for a long time, and when fourteen or fifteen Mildred had been my favorite companion. She was a little younger than I, and I liked her better than any boy I knew. Our friendship had continued through the years, but of late there had been a change in it; Mildred had become very fond of me, and her fondness seemed to have in it certain elements which annoyed me.

As a girl to make love to, no one could be better than Mildred Bronce; but I had never made love to her,—at least not earnestly,—and I did not wish that any permanent condition of loving should be established between us. Mildred did not seem to share this opinion; for every day it became plainer to me that she looked upon me as a lover, and that she was perfectly willing to return my affection.

But I had other ideas upon the subject. Into the rural town in which my family passed the greater part of the year there had recently come a young lady, Miss Janet Clinton, to whom my soul went out of my own option. In some respects, perhaps, she was not the equal of Mildred, but she was very pretty; she was small, she had a lovely mouth, was apparently of a clinging nature, and her dark eyes looked into mine with a tingling effect that no other eyes had ever produced. I was in love with her because I wished to be, and the consciousness of this fact caused me a proud satisfaction. This affair was not the result of circumstances, but of my own free will.

I wished to retain Mildred's friendship, I wished to make her happy; and with this latter intent in view I wished very much that she should not disappoint herself in her anticipations of the future.

Each year it had been my habit to make Mildred a Christmas present, and I was now looking for something to give her which would please her and suit my purpose.

When a man wishes to select a present for a lady which, while it assures her of his kind feeling toward her, will at the same time indicate that not only has he no matrimonial inclinations in her direction, but that it would be entirely unwise for her to have any such inclinations in his direction; that no matter with what degree of fondness her heart is disposed to turn toward him, his heart does not turn toward her, and that, in spite of all sentiments induced by long association and the natural fitness of things, she need never expect to be to him anything more than a sister, he has, indeed, a difficult task before him. But such was the task which I set for myself.

Day after day I wandered through the shops. I looked at odd pieces of jewelry and bric-à-brac, and at many a quaint relic or bit of art work which seemed to have a meaning, but nothing had the meaning I wanted. As to books, I found none which satisfied me; not one which was adapted to produce the exact impression that I desired.

One afternoon I was in a little basement shop kept by a fellow in a long overcoat, who, so far as I was able to judge, bought curiosities but never sold any. For some minutes I had been looking at a beautifully decorated saucer of rare workmanship for which there was no cup to match, and for which the proprietor informed me no cup could be found or manufactured. There were some points in the significance of an article of this sort, given as a present to a lady, which fitted to my purpose, but it would signify too much: I did not wish to suggest to Mildred that she need never expect to find a cup. It would be better, in fact, if I gave her anything of this kind, to send her a cup and saucer entirely unsuited to each other, and which could not, under any conditions, be used together.

I put down the saucer, and continued my search among the dusty shelves and cases.

"How would you like a paper-weight?" the shop-keeper asked. "Here is something a little odd," handing me a piece of dark-colored mineral nearly as big as my fist, flat on the under side and of a pleasing irregularity above. Around the bottom was a band of arabesque work in some dingy metal, probably German silver. I smiled as I took it.

"This is not good enough for a Christmas present," I said. "I want something odd, but it must have some value."

"Well," said the man, "that has no real value, but there is a peculiarity about it which interested me when I heard of it, and so I bought it. This mineral is a piece of what the iron-workers call shadrach. It is a portion of the iron or iron ore which passes through the smelting-furnaces without being affected by the great heat, and so they have given it the name of one of the Hebrew youths who was cast into the fiery furnace by Nebuchadnezzar, and who came out unhurt. Some people think there is a sort of magical quality about this shadrach, and that it can give out to human beings something of its power to keep their minds cool when they are in danger of being over-heated. The old gentleman who had this made was subject to fits of anger, and he thought this piece of shadrach helped to keep him from giving way to them. Occasionally he used to leave it in the house of a hot-tempered neighbor, believing that the testy individual would be cooled down for a time, without knowing how the change had been brought about. I bought a lot of things of the old gentleman's widow, and this among them. I thought I might try it some time, but I never have."

I held the shadrach in my hand, ideas concerning it rapidly flitting through my mind. Why would not this be a capital thing to give to Mildred? If it should, indeed, possess the quality ascribed to it, if it should be able to cool her liking for me, what better present could I give her? I did not hesitate long.

"I will buy this," I said; "but the ornamentation must be of a better sort. It is now too cheap and tawdry-looking."

"I can attend to that for you," said the shopkeeper. "I can have it set in a band of gold or silver filigree-work like this, if you choose."

I agreed to this proposition, but ordered the band to be made of silver, the cool tone of that metal being more appropriate to the characteristics of the gift than the warmer hues of gold.

When I gave my Christmas present to Mildred, she was pleased with it; its oddity struck her fancy.

"I don't believe anybody ever had such a paper-weight as that," she said, as she thanked me. "What is it made of?"

I told her, and explained what shadrach was; but I did not speak of its presumed influence over human beings, which, after all, might be nothing but the wildest fancy. I did not feel altogether at my ease, as I added that it was merely a trifle, a thing of no value except as a reminder of the season.

"The fact that it is a present from you gives it value," she said, as she smilingly raised her eyes to mine.

I left her house — we were all living in the city then — with a troubled conscience. What a deception I was practising upon this noble girl, who, if she did not already love me, was plainly on the point of doing so. She had received my present as if it indicated a warmth of feeling on my part, when, in fact, it was the result of a desire for a cooler feeling on her part.

But I called my reason to my aid, and I showed myself that what I had given Mildred — if it should prove to possess any virtue at all — was, indeed, a most valuable boon. It was something which would prevent the waste of her affections, the wreck of her hopes. No kindness could be truer, no regard for her happiness more sincere, than the motives which prompted me to give her the shadrach.

I did not soon again see Mildred, but now as often as possible I visited Janet. She always received me with a charming cordiality, and if this should develop into warmer sentiments I was not the man to wish to cool them. In many ways Janet seemed much better suited to me than Mildred. One of the greatest charms of this beautiful girl was a tender trustfulness, as if I were a being on whom she could lean and to whom she could look up. I liked this; it was very different from Mildred's manner: with the latter I had always been well satisfied if I felt myself standing on the same plane.

The weeks and months passed on, and again we were all in the country; and here I saw Mildred often. Our homes were not far apart, and our families were very intimate. With my opportunities for frequent observation I could not doubt that a change had come over her. She was always friendly when we met, and seemed as glad to see me as she was to see any other member of my family, but she was not the Mildred I used to know. It was plain that my existence did not make the same impression on her that it once made. She did not seem to consider it important whether I came or went; whether I was in the room or not; whether I joined a party or stayed away. All this had been very different. I knew well that Mildred had been used to consider my presence as a matter of much importance, and I now felt sure that my Christmas shadrach was doing its work. Mildred was cooling toward me. Her affection, or, to put it more modestly, her tendency to affection, was gently congealing into friendship. This was highly gratifying to my moral nature, for every day I was doing my best to warm the soul of Janet. Whether or not I succeeded in this I could not be sure; Janet was as tender and trustful and charming as ever, but no more so than she had been months before.

Sometimes I thought she was waiting for an indication of an increased warmth of feeling on my part before she allowed the temperature of her own sentiments to rise. But for one reason and another I delayed the solution of this problem. Janet was very fond of company, and although we saw a great deal of each other, we were not often alone. If we two had more frequently walked, driven, or rowed together, as Mildred and I used to do, I think Miss Clinton would soon have had every opportunity of making up her mind about the fervor of my passion.

The summer weeks passed on, and there was no change in the things which now principally concerned me, except that Mildred seemed to be growing more and more indifferent to me. From having seemed to care no more for me than for her other friends, she now seemed to care less for me than for most people. I do not mean that she showed a dislike, but she treated me with a sort of indifference which I did not fancy at all. This sort of thing had gone too far, and there was no knowing how much further it would go. It was plain enough that the shadrach was overdoing the business.

I was now in a state of much mental disquietude. Greatly as I desired to win the love of Janet, it grieved me to think of losing the generous friendship of Mildred — that friendship to which I had been accustomed for the greater part of my life, and on which, as I now discovered, I had grown to depend.

In this state of mind I went to see Mildred. I found her in the library writing. She received me pleasantly, and was sorry her father was not at home, and begged that I would excuse her finishing the note on which she was engaged, because she wished to get it into the post-office before the mail closed. I sat down on the other side of the table, and she finished her note, after which she went out to give it to a servant.

Glancing about me, I saw the shadrach. It was

partly under a litter of papers, instead of lying on them. I took it up, and was looking at it when Mildred returned. She sat down and asked me if I had heard of the changes that were to be made in the time-table of the railroad. We talked a little on the subject, and then I spoke of the shadrach, saying carelessly that it might be interesting to analyze the bit of metal; there was a little knob which might be filed off without injuring it in the least.

"You may take it," she said, "and make what experiments you please. I do not use it much; it is unnecessarily heavy for a paper-weight."

From her tone I might have supposed that she had forgotten that I had given it to her. I told her that I would be very glad to borrow the paper-weight for a time, and, putting it into my pocket, I went away, leaving her arranging her disordered papers on the table, and giving quite as much regard to this occupation as she had given to my little visit.

I could not feel sure that the absence of the shadrach would cause any diminution in the coolness of her feelings toward me, but there was reason to believe that it would prevent them from growing cooler. If she should keep that shadrach she might in time grow to hate me. I was very glad that I had taken it from her.

My mind easier on this subject, my heart turned more freely toward Janet, and, going to her house, the next day I was delighted to find her alone. She was as lovely as ever, and as cordial, but she was flushed and evidently annoyed.

"I am in a bad humor to-day," she said, "and I am

glad you came to talk to me and quiet me. Dr. Gilbert promised to take me to drive this afternoon, and we were going over to the hills where they find the wild rhododendron. I am told that it is still in blossom up there, and I want some flowers ever so much — I am going to paint them. And besides, I am crazy to drive with his new horses; and now he sends me a note to say that he is engaged."

This communication shocked me, and I began to talk to her about Dr. Gilbert. I soon found that several times she had been driving with this handsome young physician, but never, she said, behind his new horses, nor to the rhododendron hills.

Dr. Hector Gilbert was a fine young fellow, beginning practice in town, and one of my favorite associates. I had never thought of him in connection with Janet, but I could now see that he might make a most dangerous rival. When a young and talented doctor, enthusiastic in his studies, and earnestly desirous of establishing a practice, and who, if his time were not fully occupied, would naturally wish that the neighbors would think that such were the case, deliberately devotes some hours on I know not how many days to driving a young lady into the surrounding country, it may be supposed that he is really in love with her. Moreover, judging from Janet's present mood, this doctor's attentions were not without encouragement.

I went home; I considered the state of affairs; I ran my fingers through my hair; I gazed steadfastly upon the floor. Suddenly I rose. I had had an inspiration; I would give the shadrach to Dr. Gilbert.

I went immediately to the doctor's office, and found him there. He too was not in a very good humor.

"I have had two old ladies here nearly all the afternoon, and they have bored me to death," he said. "I could not get rid of them because I found they had made an appointment with each other to visit me to-day and talk over a hospital plan which I proposed some time ago and which is really very important to me, but I wish they had chosen some other time to come here. What is that thing?"

"That is a bit of shadrach," I said, "made into a paper-weight." And then I proceeded to explain what shadrach is, and what peculiar properties it must possess to resist the power of heat, which melts other metal apparently of the same class; and I added that I thought it might be interesting to analyze a bit of it and discover what fire-proof constituents it possessed.

"I should like to do that," said the doctor, attentively turning over the shadrach in his hand. "Can I take off a piece of it?"

"I will give it to you," said I, "and you can make what use of it you please. If you do analyze it, I shall be very glad indeed to hear the results of your investigations."

The doctor demurred a little at taking the paper-weight with such a pretty silver ring around it, but I assured him that the cost of the whole affair was trifling, and I should be gratified if he would take it. He accepted the gift, and was thanking me, when a patient arrived, and I departed.

I really had no right to give away this paper-weight, which, in fact, belonged to Mildred, but there are times when a man must keep his eyes on the chief good, and not think too much about other things. Besides, it was evident that Mildred did not care in the least for the bit of metal, and she had virtually given it to me.

There was another point which I took into consideration. It might be that the shadrach might simply cool Dr. Gilbert's feelings toward me, and that would be neither pleasant nor advantageous. If I could have managed matters so that Janet could have given it to him, it would have been all right. But now all that I could do was to wait and see what would happen. If only the thing would cool the doctor in a general way, that would help. He might then give more thought to his practice and his hospital ladies, and let other people take Janet driving.

About a week after this I met the doctor; he seemed in a hurry, but I stopped him. I had a curiosity to know if he had analyzed the shadrach, and asked him about it.

"No," said he; "I haven't done it. I haven't had time. I knocked off a piece of it, and I will attend to it when I get a chance. Good day."

Of course if the man was busy, he could not be expected to give his mind to a trifling matter of that sort, but I thought he need not have been so curt about it. I stood gazing after him as he walked rapidly down the street. Before I resumed my walk I saw him enter the Clinton house. Things were not going on well. The shadrach had not cooled Dr. Gilbert's feelings toward Janet.

But because the doctor was still warm in his attentions to the girl I loved, I would not in the least relax my attentions to her. I visited her as often as I could find an excuse to do so. There was generally some one else there, but Janet's disposition was of such gracious expansiveness that each one felt obliged to be satisfied with what he got, much as he may have wished for something different.

But one morning Janet surprised me. I met her at Mildred's house, where I had gone to borrow a book of reference. Although I had urged her not to put herself to so much trouble, Mildred was standing on a little ladder looking for the book, because, she said, she knew exactly what I wanted, and she was sure she could find the proper volume better than I could. Janet had been sitting in a window-seat, reading, but when I came in she put down her book and devoted herself to conversation with me. I was a little sorry for this, because Mildred was very kindly engaged in doing me a service, and I really wanted to talk to her about the book she was looking for. Mildred showed so much of her old manner this morning that I would have been very sorry to have her think that I did not appreciate her returning interest in me. Therefore, while under other circumstances I would have been delighted to talk to Janet, I did not wish to give her so much of my attention then. But Janet Clinton was a girl who insisted on people attending to her when she wished them to do so, and, having stepped through an open door into the garden, she presently called me to her. Of course I had to go.

"I will not keep you a minute from your fellow-student," she said, "but I want to ask a favor of you."

And into her dark, uplifted eyes there came a look of tender trustfulness clearer than any I had yet seen there. "Don't *you* want to drive me to the rhododendron hills?" she said. "I suppose the flowers are all gone by this time, but I have never been there, and I should like ever so much to go."

I could not help remarking that I thought Dr. Gilbert was going to take her there.

"Dr. Gilbert, indeed!" she said with a little laugh. "He promised once, and didn't come, and the next day he planned for it it rained. I don't think doctors make very good escorts, anyway, for you can't tell who is going to be sick just as you are about to start on a trip. Besides, there is no knowing how much botany I should have to hear, and when I go on a pleasure-drive I don't care very much about studying things. But of course I don't want to trouble you."

"Trouble!" I exclaimed. "It will give me the greatest delight to take you that drive or any other, and at whatever time you please."

"You are always so good and kind," she said, with her dark eyes again upraised. "And now let us go in and see if Mildred has found the book."

I spoke the truth when I said that Janet's proposition delighted me. To take a long drive with that charming girl, and at the same time to feel that she had chosen me as her companion, was a greater joy than I had yet had reason to expect; but it would have been a more satisfying joy if she had asked me in her own house and not in Mildred's; if she had not allowed the love which I hoped was growing up between her and me to interfere with the revival of the old friendship between Mildred and me.

But when we returned to the library Mildred was sitting at a table with a book before her, opened at the passage I wanted.

"I have just found it," she said with a smile. "Draw up a chair, and we will look over these maps together. I want you to show me how he travelled when he left his ship."

"Well, if you two are going to the pole," said Janet, with her prettiest smile, "I will go back to my novel."

She did not seem in the least to object to my geographical researches with Mildred, and if the latter had even noticed my willingness to desert her at the call of Janet, she did not show it. Apparently she was as much a good comrade as she had ever been. This state of things was gratifying in the highest degree. If I could be loved by Janet and still keep Mildred as my friend, what greater earthly joys could I ask?

The drive with Janet was postponed by wet weather. Day after day it rained, or the skies were heavy, and we both agreed that it must be in the bright sunshine that we would make this excursion. When we should make it, and should be alone together on the rhododendron hill, I intended to open my soul to Janet.

It may seem strange to others, and at the time it also seemed strange to me, but there was another reason besides the rainy weather which prevented my declaration of love to Janet. This was a certain nervous anxiety in regard to my friendship for Mildred. I did not in the least waver in my intention to use the best endeavors to make the one my wife, but at the same time I was oppressed by a certain alarm that in carrying out this project I might act in such a way as to wound the feelings of the other.

This disposition to consider the feelings of Mildred became so strong that I began to think that my own sentiments were in need of control. It was not right that while making love to one woman I should give so much consideration to my relations with another. The idea struck me that in a measure I had shared the fate of those who had thrown the Hebrew youths into the fiery furnace. My heart had not been consumed by the flames, but in throwing the shadrach into what I supposed were Mildred's affections it was quite possible that I had been singed by them. At any rate my conscience told me that under the circumstances my sentiments toward Mildred were too warm; in honestly making love to Janet I ought to forget them entirely.

It might have been a good thing, I told myself, if I had not given away the shadrach, but kept it as a gift from Mildred. Very soon after I reached this conclusion it became evident to me that Mildred was again cooling in my direction as rapidly as the mercury falls after sunset on a September day. This discovery did not make my mercury fall; in fact, it brought it for a time nearly to the boiling-point. I could not imagine what had happened. I almost neglected Janet, so anxious was I to know what had made this change in Mildred.

Weeks passed on, and I discovered nothing, except that Mildred had now become more than indifferent to me. She allowed me to see that my companionship did not give her pleasure.

Janet had her drive to the rhododendron hills, but she took it with Dr. Gilbert and not with me. When I heard of this it pained me, though I could not help admitting that I deserved the punishment; but my surprise was almost as great as my pain, for Janet had recently given me reason to believe that she had a very small opinion of the young doctor. In fact, she had criticised him so severely that I had been obliged to speak in his defence. I now found myself in a most doleful quandary, and there was only one thing of which I could be certain — I needed cooling toward Mildred if I still allowed myself to hope to marry Janet.

One afternoon I was talking to Mr. Bronce in his library, when, glancing toward the table used by his daughter for writing purposes, I was astounded to see, lying on a little pile of letters, the Christmas shadrach. As soon as I could get an opportunity I took it in my hand and eagerly examined it. I had not been mistaken. It was the paper-weight I had given Mildred. There was the silver band around it, and there was the place where a little piece had been knocked off by the doctor. Mildred was not at home, but I determined that I would wait and see her. I would dine with the Bronces; I would spend the evening; I would stay all night; I would not leave the house until I had had this mystery explained. She returned in about half an hour and greeted me in the somewhat stiff manner she had adopted of late; but when she noticed my perturbed expression and saw that I held the shadrach in my hand, she took a seat by the table, where for some time I had been waiting for her, alone.

"I suppose you want to ask me about that paper-weight," she remarked.

"Indeed I do," I replied. "How in the world did you happen to get it again?"

"Again?" she repeated satirically. "You may well say that. I will explain it to you. Some little time ago I called on Janet Clinton, and on her writing-desk I saw that paper-weight. I remembered it perfectly. It was the one you gave me last Christmas and afterward borrowed of me, saying that you wanted to analyze it, or something of the sort. I had never used it very much, and of course was willing that you should take it, and make experiments with it if you wanted to, but I must say that the sight of it on Janet Clinton's desk both shocked and angered me. I asked her where she got it, and she told me a gentleman had given it to her. I did not need to waste any words in inquiring who this gentleman was, but I determined that she should not rest under a mistake in regard to its proper ownership, and told her plainly that the person who had given it to her had previously given it to me; that it was mine, and he had no right to give it to any one else. 'Oh, if that is the case,' she exclaimed, 'take it, I beg of you. I don't care for it, and, what is more, I don't care any more for the man who gave it to me than I do for the thing itself.' So I took it and brought it home with me. Now you know how I happened to have it again."

For a moment I made no answer. Then I asked

her how long it had been since she had received the shadrach from Janet Clinton.

"Oh, I don't remember exactly," she said; "it was several weeks ago."

Now I knew everything; all the mysteries of the past were revealed to me. The young doctor, fervid in his desire to please the woman he loved, had given Janet this novel paper-weight. From that moment she had begun to regard his attentions with apathy, and finally — her nature was one which was apt to go to extremes — to dislike him. Mildred repossessed herself of the shadrach, which she took, not as a gift from Janet, but as her rightful property, presented to her by me. And this horrid little object, probably with renewed power, had cooled, almost frozen indeed, the sentiments of that dear girl toward me. Then, too, had the spell been taken from Janet's inclinations, and she had gone to the rhododendron hills with Dr. Gilbert.

One thing was certain. I must have that shadrach.

"Mildred," I exclaimed, "will you not give me this paper-weight? Give it to me for my own?"

"What do you want to do with it?" she asked sarcastically. "Analyze it again?"

"Mildred," said I, "I did not give it to Janet. I gave it to Dr. Gilbert, and he must have given it to her. I know I had no right to give it away at all, but I did not believe that you would care; but now I beg that you will let me have it. Let me have it for my own. I assure you solemnly I will never give it away. It has caused trouble enough already."

"I don't exactly understand what you mean by

trouble," she said, "but take it if you want it. You are perfectly welcome." And picking up her gloves and hat from the table she left me.

As I walked home my hatred of the wretched piece of metal in my hand increased with every step. I looked at it with disgust when I went to bed that night, and when my glance lighted upon it the next morning I involuntarily shrank from it, as if it had been an evil thing. Over and over again that day I asked myself why I should keep in my possession something which would make my regard for Mildred grow less and less; which would eventually make me care for her not at all? The very thought of not caring for Mildred sent a pang through my heart.

My feelings all prompted me to rid myself of what I looked upon as a calamitous talisman, but my reason interfered. If I still wished to marry Janet it was my duty to welcome indifference to Mildred.

In this mood I went out, to stroll, to think, to decide; and that I might be ready to act on my decision I put the shadrach into my pocket. Without exactly intending it I walked toward the Bronce place, and soon found myself on the edge of a pretty pond which lay at the foot of the garden. Here, in the shade of a tree, there stood a bench, and on this lay a book, an ivory paper-cutter in its leaves as marker.

I knew that Mildred had left that book on the bench; it was her habit to come to this place to read. As she had not taken the volume with her, it was probable that she intended soon to return. But then the sad thought came to me that if she saw me there she would not return. I picked up the book; I read the pages she had been reading. As I read I felt that I could think the very thoughts that she thought as she read. I was seized with a yearning to be with her, to read with her, to think with her. Never had my soul gone out to Mildred as at that moment, and yet, heavily dangling in my pocket, I carried — I could not bear to think of it. Seized by a sudden impulse, I put down the book; I drew out the shadrach, and, tearing off the silver band, I tossed the vile bit of metal into the pond.

"There!" I cried. "Go out of my possession, out of my sight! You shall work no charm on me. Let nature take its course, and let things happen as they may." Then, relieved from the weight on my heart and the weight in my pocket, I went home.

Nature did take its course, and in less than a fortnight from that day the engagement of Janet and Dr. Gilbert was announced. I had done nothing to prevent this, and the news did not disturb my peace of mind; but my relations with Mildred very much disturbed it. I had hoped that, released from the baleful influence of the shadrach, her friendly feelings toward me would return, and my passion for her had now grown so strong that I waited and watched, as a wrecked mariner waits and watches for the sight of a sail, for a sign that she had so far softened toward me that I might dare to speak to her of my love. But no such sign appeared.

I now seldom visited the Bronce house; no one of that family, once my best friends, seemed to care to see me. Evidently Mildred's feelings toward me had extended themselves to the rest of the household.

This was not surprising, for her family had long been accustomed to think as Mildred thought.

One day I met Mr. Bronce at the post-office, and, some other gentlemen coming up, we began to talk of a proposed plan to introduce a system of water-works into the village, an improvement much desired by many of us.

"So far as I am concerned," said Mr. Bronce, "I am not now in need of anything of the sort. Since I set up my steam-pump I have supplied my house from the pond at the end of my garden with all the water we can possibly want for every purpose."

"Do you mean," asked one of the gentlemen, "that you get your drinking-water in that way?"

"Certainly," replied Mr. Bronce. "The basin of the pond is kept as clean and in as good order as any reservoir can be, and the water comes from an excellent, rapid-flowing spring. I want nothing better."

A chill ran through me as I listened. The shadrach was in that pond. Every drop of water which Mildred drank, which touched her, was influenced by that demoniacal paper-weight, which, without knowing what I was doing, I had thus bestowed upon the whole Bronce family.

When I went home I made diligent search for a stone which might be about the size and weight of the shadrach, and having repaired to a retired spot I practised tossing it as I had tossed the bit of metal into the pond. In each instance I measured the distance which I had thrown the stone, and was at last enabled to make a very fair estimate of the distance to which I had thrown the shadrach when I had buried it under the waters of the pond.

That night there was a half-moon, and between eleven and twelve o'clock, when everybody in our village might be supposed to be in bed and asleep, I made my way over the fields to the back of the Bronce place, taking with me a long fish-cord with a knot in it, showing the average distance to which I had thrown the practice stone. When I reached the pond I stood as nearly as possible in the place by the bench from which I had hurled the shadrach, and to this spot I pegged one end of the cord. I was attired in an old tennis suit, and, having removed my shoes and stockings, I entered the water, holding the roll of cord in my hand. This I slowly unwound as I advanced toward the middle of the pond, and when I reached the knot I stopped, with the water above my waist.

I had found the bottom of the pond very smooth, and free from weeds and mud, and I now began feeling about with my bare feet, as I moved from side to side, describing a small arc; but I discovered nothing more than an occasional pebble no larger than a walnut.

Letting out some more of the cord, I advanced a little farther into the centre of the pond, and slowly described another arc. The water was now nearly up to my armpits, but it was not cold, though if it had been I do not think I should have minded it in the ardor of my search. Suddenly I put my foot on something hard and as big as my fist, but in an instant it moved away from under my foot; it must have been a turtle. This occurrence made me shiver a little, but I did not swerve from my purpose, and, loosing the string a little more, I went farther into the pond. The water was now nearly up to my chin, and there was something weird, mystical, and awe-inspiring in standing thus in the depths of this silent water, my eyes so near its gently rippling surface, fantastically lighted by the setting moon, and tenanted by nobody knew what cold and slippery creatures. But from side to side I slowly moved, reaching out with my feet in every direction, hoping to touch the thing for which I sought.

Suddenly I set my right foot upon something hard and irregular. Nervously I felt it with my toes. I patted it with my bare sole. It was as big as the shadrach! It felt like the shadrach. In a few moments I was almost convinced that the direful paper-weight was beneath my foot.

Closing my eyes, and holding my breath, I stooped down into the water, and groped on the bottom with my hands. In some way I had moved while stooping, and at first I could find nothing. A sensation of dread came over me as I felt myself in the midst of the dark solemn water, — around me, above me, everywhere, — almost suffocated, and apparently deserted even by the shadrach. But just as I felt that I could hold my breath no longer my fingers touched the thing that had been under my foot, and, clutching it, I rose and thrust my head out of the water. I could do nothing until I had taken two or three long breaths; then, holding up the object in my hand to the light of the expiring moon, I saw that it was like the shadrach; so like, indeed, that I felt that it must be it.

Turning, I made my way out of the water as rapidly as possible, and, dropping on my knees on the ground, I tremblingly lighted the lantern which I had left on the bench, and turned its light on the thing I had found. There must be no mistake; if this was not the shadrach I would go in again. But there was no necessity for re-entering the pond; it *was* the shadrach.

With the extinguished lantern in one hand and the lump of mineral evil in the other, I hurried home. My wet clothes were sticky and chilly in the night air. Several times in my haste I stumbled over clods and briers, and my shoes, which I had not taken time to tie, flopped up and down as I ran. But I cared for none of these discomforts; the shadrach was in my power.

Crossing a wide field I heard, not far away, the tramping of hoofs, as of a horseman approaching at full speed. I stopped and looked in the direction of the sound. My eyes had now become so accustomed to the dim light that I could distinguish objects somewhat plainly, and I quickly perceived that the animal that was galloping toward me was a bull. I well knew what bull it was; this was Squire Starling's pasture-field, and that was his great Alderney bull, Ramping Sir John of Ramapo II.

I was well acquainted with that bull, renowned throughout the neighborhood for his savage temper and his noble pedigree — son of Ramping Sir John of Rampo I., whose sire was the Great Rodolphin, son of Prince Maximus of Granby, one of whose daughters averaged eighteen pounds of butter a week, and who, himself, had killed two men.

The bull, who had not perceived me when I crossed the field before, for I had then made my way with as little noise as possible, was now bent on punishing my intrusion upon his domains, and bellowed as he came on. I was in a position of great danger. With my flopping shoes it was impossible to escape by flight; I must stand and defend myself. I turned and faced the furious creature, who was not twenty feet distant, and then, with all my strength, I hurled the shadrach, which I held in my right hand, directly at his shaggy forehead. My ability to project a missile was considerable, for I had held, with credit, the position of pitcher in a base-ball nine, and as the shadrach struck the bull's head with a great thud, he stopped as if he had suddenly run against a wall.

I do not know that actual and violent contact with the physical organism of a recipient accelerates the influence of a shadrach upon the mental organism of said recipient, but I do know that the contact of my projectile with that bull's skull instantly cooled the animal's fury. For a few moments he stood and looked at me, and then his interest in me as a man and trespasser appeared to fade away, and, moving slowly from me, Ramping Sir John of Ramapo II. began to crop the grass.

I did not stop to look for the shadrach; I considered it safely disposed of. So long as Squire Starling used that field for a pasture, connoisseurs in mineral fragments would not be apt to wander through it, and when it should be ploughed, the shadrach, to ordinary eyes no more than a common stone, would be buried beneath the sod. I awoke the next morning refreshed and happy, and none the worse for my wet walk.

"Now," I said to myself, "nature shall truly have her own way. If the uncanny comes into my life and that of those I love, it shall not be brought in by me."

About a week after this I dined with the Bronce family. They were very cordial, and it seemed to me the most natural thing in the world to be sitting at their table. After dinner Mildred and I walked together in the garden. It was a charming evening, and we sat down on the bench by the edge of the pond. I spoke to her of some passages in the book I had once seen there.

"Oh, have you read that?" she asked with interest.

"I have seen only two pages of it," I said, "and those I read in the volume you left on this bench, with a paper-cutter in it for a marker. I long to read more and talk with you of what I have read."

"Why, then, didn't you wait? You might have known that I would come back."

I did not tell her that I knew that because I was there she would not have come. But before I left the bench I discovered that hereafter, wherever I might be, she was willing to come and to stay.

Early in the next spring Mildred and I were married, and on our wedding trip we passed through a mining district in the mountains. Here we visited one of the great ironworks, and were both much interested in witnessing the wonderful power of man, air, and fire over the stubborn king of metals.

"What is this substance?" asked Mildred of one

of the officials who was conducting us through the works.

"That," said the man, "is what we call shad—"

"My dear," I cried, "we must hurry away this instant or we shall lose the train. Come; quick; there is not a moment for delay." And with a word of thanks to the guide I seized her hand and led her, almost running, into the open air.

Mildred was amazed.

"Never before," she exclaimed, "have I seen you in such a hurry. I thought the train we decided to take did not leave for at least an hour."

"I have changed my mind," I said, "and think it will be a great deal better for us to take the one which leaves in ten minutes."

THE REVEREND EZEKIEL CRUMP

IT was one o'clock on a bright October day, and Mr. Nathan Rinkle had just sat down to dinner, with Mrs. Nicely Lent on the other side of the table. The day was warm for the season, and Mr. Rinkle, having been very busy since early morning, had a good appetite. But he had barely made one deep cut in the leg of mutton before him, when the door opened, and a boy came in with an old straw hat in his hand. He hesitated for a moment as if he thought he should make some apology for breaking in upon the sanctity of the dinner hour, and then he said: —

"I've just come to tell you that I think the Rev'rend Ezekiel Crump is dyin'. He's all doubled up."

"Gracious!" exclaimed Mr. Rinkle, suddenly pushing back his chair, "I must go out this minute! It's the heat. I didn't count on it's bein' so extra warm to-day." And with this, he clapped on his hat and left the house.

"Oh dear!" exclaimed Mrs. Lent as she gazed at the table which she had arranged with so much care. "I suppose I might as well put these things by the fire to keep 'em warm. There's no knowin' when he'll be back. I wish that boy Joe had kept away until dinner was over. But I suppose it couldn't be helped. It would never do to let the Reverend Ezekiel Crump die."

Nathan Rinkle was a florist, and the Reverend Ezekiel Crump was a new and fine pelargonium which had been originated by Mr. Rinkle himself, and which he had named for the reverend gentleman who had married his father and mother and baptized him. Mr. Rinkle had often said that this good man's name would be given to the finest new flower he should ever grow; and as he did not believe he should produce anything better than this pelargonium, the name was given to it.

Nathan was a tall, slim, muscular bachelor of about forty, industrious, and devoted to his profession, and a respected member of society in the country region in which he lived. Mrs. Lent, a well-nurtured lady, whose age hovered around thirty-five, was the widow of Mr. Rinkle's former partner. The house belonged to Mr. Rinkle, and he, with Joshua Lent and his wife, had lived in it very pleasantly and profitably five or six years. When Joshua died three years ago this autumn, Nathan was not the man to turn his widow out of doors; so Mrs. Lent, who now owned a certain share in the business, remained as housekeeper and general domestic manager. And, thus far, the arrangement had been found pleasant and profitable to all parties concerned.

It was half an hour before Mr. Rinkle returned from the greenhouse, and as Mrs. Lent had seen him coming, the dinner was again on the table when he entered.

"It wasn't as bad as Joe thought it was," he said as he took his seat at the table, "but it was bad enough. I think I have been too careful with that plant, a little too careful. I've been sparing with the water on it. I didn't want it to bloom too fast. I wanted the three sprays I left on it to be absolutely perfect for the flower show to-morrow, and I was so busy this morning gettin' the other things ready I didn't look at the Rev'rend Ezekiel, and as he was in a pretty hot place for such a day, and too dry about the roots, he began to wilt. But I think he is all right now. I've given him a good soakin' and put him in the shade, and he began to brighten up before I left him. I tell you, Mrs. Lent, that gave me a real shock."

"As well it might," said the sympathetic Nicely.

That afternoon Mrs. Lent went out to the greenhouses to look at the wonderful new pelargonium. She found the reverend gentleman fully restored to health, strength, and beauty, and she felt quite convinced that never had the eye of man rested upon so grand and glorious a pelargonium. And furthermore, there could be no imaginable reason to doubt that on the morrow Mr. Rinkle would receive a first prize.

When Mr. Rinkle, with his lantern, came in from the greenhouses that evening, he told Mrs. Lent that he should go out several times during the night to see if everything was all right; and that he should leave very early in the morning for the town about ten miles away where the flower show was to be held. "I'm going to send Joe off with one wagon at daylight, and then, as soon as I can get off, I shall follow with the other wagon, which won't be more than half full; so I'm goin' to stop at the Widow Sharp's and take along the plants she's got to show, for she hasn't any way of gettin' them there herself."

"Do you mean," asked Nicely, somewhat anxiously, "that you are going before breakfast?"

"Oh, yes," said Nathan; "and as I've got to stop at the Widow Sharp's anyway, I'll breakfast there."

"And I suppose, of course, that you'll take Rev'rend Ezekiel Crump with you?"

"Oh, yes, indeed," answered Nathan. "You may be sure that I'll take charge of that plant. That pelargonium is going to make a commotion at the show I can tell you. I've got a lot of young plants of it, but I didn't expect I'd have one in bloom this year. This one is a little spindlin', it is true, but he has got three sprays of flowers which are finer than anybody has ever yet seen on a pelargonium plant."

"I am so glad," said Mrs. Lent, "that you are able to exhibit it so much sooner than you expected to. That ought to be a good thing for you."

"I've no doubt it will be," said Nathan, taking up his candle.

"I'll leave Gottlieb Stein in charge of the greenhouses to-morrow, and I'll tell him to come up to the house now and then to see if you want anything. He'll come to work at seven o'clock, and I'll see him before I go. Good night."

In the early dawn of the next morning, the boy Joe started for the show with the gray mare and a well-loaded wagon; and at seven o'clock Nathan Rinkle began to be impatient for the coming of his chief assistant,

Gottlieb Stein, who lived about a mile away. He wanted him to put the brown horse to the covered wagon, in a back corner of which the Reverend Ezekiel Crump was to travel, carefully protected from the cool morning air; and he had many directions to give his assistant for the conduct of his establishment during the day. It was seldom that Gottlieb was late in coming to his work, and Nathan was much annoyed that he should happen to be so on this most important occasion.

After fuming and fretting for at least a quarter of an hour as he walked up and down the principal greenhouse, gathering together the plants he intended to take to the show, the thought struck him that possibly Gottlieb might have forgotten what was to be the great business of the day, and had gone to work in some of the other houses. So he hastily ran out to look for him. Nathan opened the doors of two other greenhouses, looked in and called, but the man was not in either of them; then he ran over to the violet house, which was newer than the other buildings and at some distance from them. Mr. Rinkle did not find there the man he wanted to see, but he found something he did not want to see, and that was that a number of the violet beds were very much in need of water.

"Confound it!" he ejaculated. "Here is a piece of forgetfulness. And while I'm waiting for that fellow I might as well be freshening up these beds." And taking up a watering-pot he proceeded to the cistern.

This reservoir, supplied with rain-water from the roof, was simply a wide hole in the central part of the house about nine feet deep. It had been dug in a bed of clay, and the inside of it had not yet been walled up or cemented, for as Mr. Rinkle had found that its clay sides and bottom were impervious to water, and it made a very good cistern as it was, for the present he had postponed finishing it. As the cistern was yet uncovered no pump had been placed in it, and Gottlieb had found it easy enough to draw water from it by means of a bucket and rope. So now, as he had to take Gottlieb's place, Nathan Rinkle crouched down to the edge of the cistern and lowered the bucket. Gottlieb Stein was a heavy-footed man, and had crouched at that spot so often that the earth was a little depressed and inclined cisternward, and Mr. Rinkle's overshoes being wet with the morning dew were slippery. In consequence, before the bucket was half-way down, Mr. Rinkle slipped into the cistern himself, and arrived with a great splash at the bottom. Plunged thus suddenly into darkness and water the good gardener's surprise almost took away his breath. Fortunately, he came down in a standing position, and as soon as he was able to command his senses he discovered that, although a good deal jarred, he had not been hurt. He also discovered, to his great surprise, that the water was very low, and that it did not come up to the top of the rubber overshoes which he wore to protect the well-blacked boots he had put on for the flower show. The season had been dry, and but little rain had run into the cistern, and it might be that the difficulty of dipping with a bucket in two or three inches of water would explain Gottlieb's remissness in the matter of watering the violets.

Nathan's first impulse was to wade around the sides of the cistern and endeavor to find some means of climbing out. This was instinctively natural, but impossible. The walls, although not quite perpendicular, were smooth and slippery.

Then, at the top of his voice, Nathan began to call for help, but after indulging in this exercise for some time he was forced to admit to himself that it was useless. The door of the violet house was shut, and as it was at a considerable distance from any other building, it was not at all likely that he could make anybody hear him until Gottlieb, not finding his employer anywhere else, should come to that building to look for him.

Nathan's anger more than filled the cistern. He was not a swearing man, but if the dilatory Gottlieb could have heard the threats of his employer and could have seen the clenched fist he shook in the air, he would probably have been afraid to go to his assistance. But as he could do nothing but wait, Nathan thought he might wait as comfortably as possible, so he laid hold of the bucket, and, turning it bottom upward, sat down upon it. He drew his coat-tails over his knees, and as his feet were protected by his overshoes, he was enabled to sit thus without getting wet.

It was not cold in the cistern for the air was tempered by the greenhouse atmosphere above, and although it was very damp, Mr. Rinkle did not mind that. He had passed so many years of his life in moist glass houses, going from their heat out into the cold and dampness of the outer air without any change of clothing, that his skin had become tough and hardened, and he never thought of such a thing as taking cold. As he sat thus and considered his misfortunes he was still very angry, but he did not despair. Even if Gottlieb did not make his appearance until eight o'clock it would be time enough for him to start with his flowers for the show; and so he sat and sat until, as his sleep had been very much broken the night before, he fell into a doze. With his hands folded in his lap, and his chin on his breast, he slept as he had often done during the night watches in his greenhouses.

While Mr. Rinkle slept Mrs. Nicely Lent was at work in her kitchen. She was a pleasant-looking woman of a cheerful temperament, and yet as she worked she heaved a little sigh. Her breakfast was over and she was preparing the mince meat for the first mince pie of the season, and was doing it with great care, for Mr. Rinkle was fond of mince pies and would gladly welcome this unexpected harbinger of the season of good eating.

Moreover, it was Mrs. Lent's birthday, and she saw no better way of celebrating it than in making something good for Mr. Rinkle. It was quite certain that no one would think of making anything good for her. In no way was it a very joyful anniversary, for it is lonelier to be lonely on one's birthday than on any other day. Even her little maid Elizabeth was absent on a visit to her parents, and Gottlieb, whose own good nature — even if Mr. Rinkle had not told him to do so — should have prompted him to come to the house to see if he were needed, had not made his appearance.

"I suppose," thought Mrs. Nicely, "that Mr. Rinkle had a good breakfast at Mrs. Sharp's, for she expected him, and it may be — for she is quite forward enough for that sort of thing — that she has persuaded him to take her to the flower show." And here there came a little sigh. "But if he's done that he's done it," she reflected, "and there's no help for it. But I shall put off dinner, and won't have it till he comes home, and then he shall have his mince pie, nice and hot, as he likes it."

She was turning over the mince meat with a fork, looking for such pieces of suet as might be large enough to be picked out. "Mince pies do not agree with him very well," she said to herself, "but he is very fond of them, and I will take out as much suet as I can and put in a little more brandy. I don't think he will notice it, and it will make them more wholesome."

Her fork now brought up a large raisin, and she held it for a moment, thinking it might be better to cut it in half before putting it back. Mr. Rinkle was very fond of raisins, but to agree with him they ought to be thoroughly cooked. Nicely Lent was a woman who had tender sympathies and pleasant memories, and, as she sat with the raisin still upon her fork, she thought of other birthdays that had been so different from this. She did not mind on ordinary mornings being left alone in the house, but this morning it was indeed depressing to be there without a soul to speak to her. She could imagine Mr. Rinkle in all the brightness and gladness of the flower show; she could hear the delightful admiration provoked by the Reverend Ezekiel Crump, in whom she felt almost a maternal pride; and she thought, with a pang, that perhaps the Widow Sharp was at that moment making herself officious by dilating to the bystanders upon the merits of this grand pelargonium. And here was she, sitting alone in her kitchen! As she thought thus, and of her other birthdays, a large tear trickled down her cheek and dropped upon the raisin.

This aroused her to a sense of the present. It would not do to put a raisin that had been cried upon into a pie, and she was about to throw it away. But she hesitated; that tear had been evoked by sweet memories of the past. It seemed like a sacrilege to throw it away. She took the raisin gently from the fork, and, going to the window, made a little hole in the mould of a pot of mignonette which Mr. Rinkle had given her, and buried the raisin therein. It suited her to think that the little rootlets of the mignonette would take up that tear. She put her nose to the delicate blossoms of the plant and then she returned to her work.

If Mrs. Lent had known that the day before had been Gottlieb Stein's birthday, and that he was now in bed at home sleeping off the effects of a large supper, which in honor of the anniversary had been given to some chosen friends, she would have hastened to the greenhouses to see if they needed any attention in regard to warmth or ventilation; and she would have discovered Mr. Rinkle's sorry plight, and her hands would have borne him a ladder.

If Mr. Rinkle had known of Gottlieb's birthday supper and its consequences he would not so frequently and with such drowsy content have renewed his naps, thinking each time that he half opened his eyes that they had been closed but for a minute or two, and not imagining that his nature was repaying itself the several hours of sleep of which he had deprived it the night before.

It was nearly noon when along a path which led from a handsome house upon a hillside half a mile away a young lady appeared walking briskly toward the Rinkle greenhouses. A more charming girl is seldom seen on a bright October morning, or, indeed, upon any other morning.

At this same time there walked along the crest of the hills on the other side of the narrow valley in which the greenhouses lay a young man with a stick under his arm, who had started out for a long country tramp. But as he turned his head to gaze upon the bright autumnal scenery beneath him he suddenly stopped.

"Upon my word," he exclaimed aloud, "I believe that is Clara. Yes, truly, it is she. She is going down to Nathan Rinkle's greenhouses. What glorious good luck. I wonder if I can get there before her."

There was really no doubt upon this subject, for the young man ran down the hill, vaulted over a fence, crossed a brook, and, hurrying through the Rinkle apple orchard, reached the nearest greenhouse in a surprisingly short time. He had been there for nearly five minutes, walking up and down, smelling some flowers without perceiving their scent, and looking at others without noticing their color, when the door opened and the young lady entered. His astute mind had rightly divined that she would go into the house first reached by the path.

With outstretched hand he advanced to meet her, and took no pains to conceal his delight in doing so. She was surprised, and all the prettier for that.

"I have come," she said, as she offered him her hand, "to get this basket filled with flowers. But Mr. Rinkle is not here, I believe."

"No," said the young man. "Will you wait for him here, or shall we go and look for him?"

"Oh, I will go and look for him," she said, "but don't let me trouble you, Mr. Hatfield."

"Trouble!" he exclaimed. "As if it were possible." And they went out together.

Young Leonard Hatfield was not the avowed lover of Miss Knightley, but the only reason for this was that he had never yet had an opportunity of avowing his passion for her. He had adored her for what seemed to him a very long time, but never in her father's mansion on the hill, on the tennis-grounds, or in the houses of friends, had he found the moment he had longed for. Now it seemed to him that it had come. He would have been glad to open his heart to her in that quiet greenhouse among the flowers, but she was in such a hurry to leave it she gave him no time.

The two now entered the next greenhouse, but they found no one there. Leonard was in favor of waiting there until some one came, but Clara would not agree to that; she thought it better to go find some one.

They now went into the principal greenhouse, and near the door stood a number of plants covered with beautiful blossoms, and prominent among these was the Reverend Ezekiel Crump.

Clara was a great lover of flowers. "What a perfectly beautiful pelargonium this is!" she exclaimed. "Oh, if I could have one of those sprays. I wish I could find some one to attend to me."

"I don't think Mr. Rinkle or any of his men are here," said Leonard, after walking to the other end of the house and calling several times, "but here is some one who can attend to you. Let me cut off this spray and give it to you. I shall be so glad to do it," and he took a knife from his pocket.

"Oh, no, no," exclaimed Clara, stretching out her hand toward him. "You must not do it, I am sure that this is a rare flower, and very likely Mr. Rinkle intends to take it to the flower show at Marston, which opens to-day."

"Oh no," said Leonard, quite confidently. "He has taken his flowers there long before this. I have no doubt he had a lot of this sort of pelargonium,—more than he wanted, and he left this one."

Clara was examining the flower with great interest. "I must find out about this," she said. "I never saw anything like it. Just look at this spray with five great blossoms on it, each of them nearly three inches in diameter! And what exquisite blending of crimson, pink, and cream. I wonder what it is called." She stooped and read the name of the plant which was written on a wooden label stuck into the earth of the pot. "How utterly absurd!" she exclaimed, laughing. "This perfectly beautiful thing is named the Reverend Ezekiel Crump."

She laughed again, and Leonard laughed with her. But he did not intend to waste his time in merriment; his mind was bent on earnest work. Here was a chance to speak which he must not lose.

"Miss Knightley," he said, "if you will accept from me this new and most beautiful flower, it will give me a pleasure as new and beautiful as —"

"Oh, you mustn't do it," she cried. "Don't touch it, please. I must ask Mr. Rinkle about it, or his man, if he isn't here." And, without further words, she turned and left the house.

Leonard followed her, disappointed and annoyed. Miss Knightley's abrupt manner showed him that she did not wish to give him the opportunity to speak to her of the new and beautiful pleasure to which he had alluded. But he did not intend to give up the attempt, and he was quickly at her side.

"There is only one other place they can be," she said, "they must be in the violet house."

Leonard did not wish to hurry to the violet house, or to any other house where they might expect to find people.

"Miss Knightley," said he, "suppose we go there by this broad walk which leads around the gardens. That footpath is very narrow, and may be wet."

"Oh, this leads straight to the house," said she, "and that one goes ever so far around." And she immediately took the narrow footwalk.

When following a lady along a path wide enough for only one, and bordered by tall grass and bushes, it is not often convenient to propose marriage to her, especially if she be walking very fast. But Leonard followed Miss Knightley resolutely. If it were necessary he would walk home with her.

This day he would certainly finish what he had begun to say to her.

"I declare," said Miss Knightly, when she had proceeded nearly to the middle of the violet house, "there is nobody here. I certainly expected to find some one in this place."

"And most happy am I," said Leonard, stepping close to her, "that there is nobody here; for this gives me a chance to tell you, Clara, that I love you; for, with all my heart and soul, I have long loved you, and I cannot wait any longer to tell you so." In his excitement he took hold of her left hand, her right being occupied with her basket.

Mr. Rinkle awakened when he heard the door of the violet house open. In an instant he was sitting up alert, and with every sense at its sharpest. "It must be after eight o'clock," he said to himself, "and that rascal has just come. I'll pay him well for this. But I'll wait until he comes nearer, and first give him a good fright."

Prepared to give a howl which might come from a wild demon of the depths, Nathan sat, leaning forward and ready to spring to his feet when the miscreant Gottlieb should be near enough. But, suddenly, his mood changed. "There are the footsteps of two persons," he thought, "and I hear the rustling of a dress. One must be a woman." Then hearing Clara's exclamation his heart sank. "It is Miss Knightley," he said to himself, "and some one with her. Oh, dear me, I must not let them know I am here. If she should go home and tell her father she found me down a cistern I'd never hear the end of it. He'd laugh at me as long as he lives." So, crouching down as low as possible, Mr. Rinkle remained perfectly quiet, hoping that these untimely visitors might soon leave the house. But the next moment he heard Leonard's avowal of his love.

"My conscience," thought Nathan, holding his breath in amazement. "It's that young Hatfield making love to her. How very embarrassing. Oh dear! Oh dear! It would be awful if they knew I was so close to them." But, in spite of his embarrassment, Nathan did not put his fingers in his ears. His heart had never beat so quickly; he had never been more interested.

Leonard continued: "Clara," he said, speaking earnestly and rapidly, "may I love you? Can I hope that you will love me! Oh, do not think of going away. There is nothing in the world so important as what I am saying to you."

Clara had looked toward the door, but whether she contemplated a retreat to it, or whether she glanced through its glass panes in the fear that some one might be approaching, Leonard could not tell; but she saw no one, and it was impossible to retreat, so tightly was her hand held. She turned her head from the door, and bent her eyes on the ground.

"Oh, Clara!" he exclaimed, "will you not speak to me? Will you not look at me?"

She did not speak, but she looked up at him. That was enough.

"How very embarrassing," thought Mr. Rinkle, his ears expanding like opening calla lilies, and his heart beating faster in his excited interest. "She must have agreed, for they surely are kissin'. Yes, I can hear 'em, and most likely huggin'. Mercy on me! It's lucky they don't know I'm here. How dreadful it would be if they should even hear me breathe!" And as this thought came to him he pressed his lips tightly together.

"Oh happy, happy day!" cried Leonard. "Oh glorious world! Oh darling Clara — my own forever."

"Dear me! Dear me!" thought Mr. Rinkle. "How warmed up he is! And I'm not surprised. I wonder if he really is holdin' her in his arms. Yes, he must be. That was another kiss."

Some calla lilies are so large that it was impossible for Mr. Rinkle's ears to rival their dimensions, but they did their best.

"And you really are mine — forever and always?" asked the ardent lover.

And into the violet-perfumed air of the greenhouse there was breathed the one word "Yes."

"There," thought Mr. Rinkle, "that is the first thing she has said. But, to be sure, he hasn't given her much chance. What! Again and again! I almost wish they would go away. This is getting to be very embarrassing."

"Come, darling," said Leonard, "let us go. And nothing shall now prevent my giving that loveliest flower to the loveliest woman on earth. It shall be my first present to her, and a fit one. She shall carry home my love, and with it the finest spray of blossoms from the Reverend Ezekiel Crump."

"Don't you do it!" screamed Mr. Rinkle, springing to his feet. "Don't you touch it! I'm going to take that flower to the show. I wouldn't have it spoiled for the world."

There was a scream from Clara; a shout from Leonard. Then the young lady began to tremble, and sat down on the floor. Her lover assisted her to lean back against one of the supports of the violet beds, and then, seeing that she had not really fainted, he sprang to the open mouth of the cistern. There, a little below the surface of the floor, he saw the pale face of Mr. Rinkle, who was standing on the bucket.

"I beg a thousand pardons, Mr. Hatfield," said the trembling florist, dismayed at what he had done, "and I vow to you that I wouldn't have heard a word you've been sayin' if it had been possible for me to sink any deeper into the bowels of the earth. There is a ladder at the far end of the greenhouse, and if you'll put that down here, Mr. Hatfield, I'll come up and tell you all about it."

Leonard was so amazed, so shocked, and so angry that he could find no words in which to reply to this apparition in the cistern, but he brought the ladder, and very soon the florist was standing before him and Clara, who had now risen to her feet.

"This is very embarrassing," said Mr. Rinkle, his hands clasped before him.

"Now then," cried Leonard, fiercely, "none of that nonsense. I got you out to hear what you had to say about this contemptible piece of business."

Mr. Rinkle looked first at the angry young man and then at the pale Clara, and told everything just as it had happened. "You see," said he in conclusion, "I kept so very quiet, thinkin' to frighten Gottlieb, that you two began speakin' in a way that might be called confidential before I had time to let you know there was some one else in the greenhouse; and then I didn't like to speak out because I knew it would embarrass you so dreadfully, and I felt at any moment you might be on the p'int of goin' away. As for me, I assure you I never was so embarrassed since the beginning of my days."

"Look here," exclaimed Leonard, "I want to know if you heard everything we said?"

"Oh, no, indeed!" replied the good Nathan. "There were times when I couldn't hear a word. You see, I was at the very bottom of the cistern. But of course I couldn't help understandin' the drift of the conversation, which seemed in a way to betoken that you two were engaged to be married."

Miss Knightley, whose color had come back to her face, looked at Leonard; he looked at her, and they both laughed. Mr. Rinkle saw his opportunity and extended a hand to each. "Let me congratulate you," he said; "and I beg from the bottom of my heart that you won't mind an old fellow like me gettin' by the merest accident a hint of your engagement before anybody else. And you may trust me for never sayin' a word to a livin' soul about it; as far as that goes it might have been one of them pots that was down the cistern."

There was a moment of silence, and Clara was the first to speak.

"It is dreadfully embarrassing, as you say, Mr. Rinkle, but it can't be helped now, and I am willing to forgive you. But you must promise not only not to mention our engagement until we are ready ourselves to announce it, but that you will never, never to the end of your days, mention to a living soul that you were anywhere near at the time it was made."

"Oh, bless me!" cried Mr. Rinkle. "I'll never do that. It would make me the laughing stock of the county."

"If I ever hear," said Leonard, "that this has leaked out I shall make it my business that the people in this neighborhood shall never go into one of your greenhouses without sending somebody ahead to see who is in the cistern."

"Oh, you need have no fear of that," said Nathan. "And now you must excuse me for leaving you so abruptly. I must hurry off to the flower show. I haven't my watch with me, but it must be a good deal after eight o'clock."

"After eight," exclaimed Leonard, taking out his watch. "It is half-past twelve."

Mr. Rinkle stood aghast. "I must have slept the whole morning," he said, wofully. "And that settles me at the flower show. The prizes were to be given out at noon to-day, while things are fresh, and there is no use in my thinking of going there at this time. It is all up with me and my exhibition, at least the best part of it."

An idea suddenly struck the florist. "Stay here, please," he said, "I'll be back in a minute." And he ran out of the house.

In a short time he returned bearing in his hand the largest spray of blossoms from the Reverend Ezekiel Crump. "It's no use lettin' 'em stay on till they're withered," he said, "and as the plant can't enter for a prize now, I'll let you, Mr. Hatfield, do what you wanted to do, and give your lady a flower that no other lady ever had before. If you knew how I'd worked and waited to get those blossoms, you'd know the value of them."

This extinguished the last spark of resentment in Leonard's mind, and Mr. Rinkle considerately absented himself during the presentation of the flowers.

It was evening; dinner was over, and Mr. Rinkle pushed back his chair with an air of great content. At his hasty luncheon, which he ate standing, and in a perturbation of mind quite natural after what had happened, he had merely stated to Mrs. Lent that he had not gone to the flower show because Gottlieb had not come to take charge. But now, during the dinner, he had given Mrs. Lent a full account of his misadventures, alluding to his rescue from the cistern only by saying that Mr. Hatfield had happened to come into the violet house and had helped him out.

"That was a wonderfully good mince pie, Mrs. Lent," he remarked, in his after-dinner serenity. "There was never a better."

"If I had only known," said Mrs. Lent, "that while I was making it you were down in that dreadful hole how fast I would have run to you."

Mr. Rinkle crossed his legs and smiled. He was in a state of great good humor. "I know you would,

Mrs. Lent, I know you would. But, after all, perhaps it's just as well you didn't come."

She looked surprised. "Don't you think I could have helped you out as well as anybody?"

"Of course you could. I wasn't thinking of that," said Nathan, walking up and down the floor, and still smiling. Suddenly he struck his hands together, and then he took his hat from its peg. "Mrs. Lent," said he, "don't clear away the dinner things. I'll be back in a minute."

When he returned he brought with him the second largest spray of flowers from the Reverend Ezekiel Crump, bearing four great blossoms.

"Nicely," said he, "allow me to present to the loveliest woman on earth, the loveliest flower, at least of the pelargonium family, that was ever grown by man."

Mrs. Lent stood up amazed. Never before had he called her Nicely; and what did he mean by bringing her that almost sacred flower? "I don't understand," she gasped.

"Nicely," he said, "may I love you? Will you love me in return? Come now, don't look down or think about doing kitchen work. There is nothing so important as what I am saying to you."

She understood now. Flushing and trembling she could not speak, but she looked up at him, and that was enough. As for Nathan, he forgot nothing of the lesson that he had learned.

It was an hour afterward. The room was in order, and the two were sitting before the fire. He had just finished giving her a full account of the interview he had overheard between Miss Knightley and Mr. Hatfield. "Of course I wouldn't have told you," he said, "so long as we were merely two good friends, but now that we are the same as one, I couldn't help tellin' you. It's your right to know all I know."

The widow was so well aware of Nathan's desire to tell things about people that a faint suspicion came into her mind that perhaps he had proposed to her because there was no other way in which he could justify himself in telling her this wonderful bit of news. But she dismissed the thought as an unworthy one.

"After all," exclaimed the jubilant Nathan, "the Reverend Ezekiel Crump brought me a prize. He brought me you."

Mrs. Lent looked at him inquiringly. "What had he to do with it?" she said.

He turned a beaming face toward her. "Nicely," said he, "if them two had gone away without knowing I was in the cistern, and I'd had to wait till Gottlieb came and got me out, and that rascal didn't show himself till two o'clock this afternoon, there'd been a fight; and as he is a big fellow, and I'd been a fiery mad one, I wouldn't have been in a fit state this day to make love to anybody. But it was the name of the Reverend Ezekiel Crump that brought me bouncin' to my feet and got me out of that hole, while I was in such a state of mind from hearin' what I heard, and thinkin' about what I imagined that I was one tingle of glowin' excitement from my head that was in the air to my feet that were in the water, and I kept thinkin' and thinkin' about it, till early in the afternoon I made up my mind that as soon as I could get the day's work done and dinner was over, I wouldn't wait any longer to declare my love, just as young Hatfield couldn't wait any longer to declare his."

"Nathan," said she, "did hearing those two talk put this disposition into you?"

He threw one arm over the back of her chair. "No, indeed, Nicely," he answered, "it only brought it out."

The next day Mr. Rinkle went to the flower show dressed in his best clothes, and wearing in his buttonhole the remaining spray of blossoms from his new pelargonium. His brother florists stared with amazement at his adornment. "If you had brought yesterday the plant that bore that flower," one of them exclaimed, "you would have gained a first prize."

"Oh I got prize enough," said Nathan, with an air of superiority to floricultural distinctions, "and the Reverend Ezekiel Crump must wait till next year for his turn."

Norwood Press:
J. S. Cushing & Co. — Berwick & Smith.
Boston, Mass., U.S.A.

BRIEF LIST of Books of Fiction Published by Charles Scribner's Sons, 743-745 Broadway, New York.

William Waldorf Astor.

Valentino: An Historical Romance. 12mo, $1.00. **Sforza:** A Story of Milan. 12mo, $1.50.

"The story is full of clear-cut little tableaux of mediæval Italian manners, customs and observances. The movement throughout is spirited, the reproduction of bygone times realistic. Mr. Astor has written a romance which will heighten the reputation he made by 'Valentino.'"—*The New York Tribune.*

Arlo Bates.

A Wheel of Fire. 12mo, paper, 50 cts.; cloth, $1.00.

"The novel deals with character rather than incident, and is evolved from one of the most terrible of moral problems with a subtlety not unlike that of Hawthorne."—*The Critic.*

Hjalmar H. Boyesen.

Falconberg. Illustrated. 12mo, $1.50. **Gunnar.** Sq. 12mo, paper, 50 cts.; cloth, $1.25. **Tales from Two Hemispheres.** Sq. 12mo, $1.00. **Ilka on the Hill Top,** and Other Stories. Sq. 12mo, $1.00. **Queen Titania.** Sq. 12mo, $1.00. **Social Strugglers.** 12mo, $1.25.

"Mr. Boyesen's stories possess a sweetness, a tenderness and a drollery that are fascinating, and yet they are no more attractive than they are strong."—*The Home Journal.*

H. C. Bunner.

The Story of a New York House. Illustrated by A. B. Frost. 12mo, $1.25. **The Midge.** 12mo, paper, 50 cts.; cloth, $1.00. **Zadoc Pine,** and Other Stories. 12mo, paper, 50 cts.; cloth, $1.00.

"It is Mr. Bunner's delicacy of touch and appreciation of what is literary art that give his writings distinctive quality. Everything Mr. Bunner paints shows the happy appreciation of an author who has not alone mental discernment, but the artistic appreciation. The author and the artist both supplement one another in this excellent 'Story of a New York House.'"—*The New York Times.*

Frances Hodgson Burnett.

That Lass O' Lowrie's. Illustrated. Paper, 50 cts.; cloth, $1 25. **Haworth's.** Illustrated. 12mo, $1.25. **Through One Administration.** 12mo, $1.50. **Louisiana.** 12mo, $1.25. **A Fair Barbarian.** 12mo, paper, 50 cts.; cloth, $1.25. **Vagabondia:** A Love Story. 12mo, paper, 50 cts.; cloth, $1.25. **Surly Tim,** and Other Stories. 12mo, $1.25. **Earlier Stories.** First Series. **Earlier Stories.** Second Series. 12mo, each, paper, 50 cts.; cloth, $1.25. **The Pretty Sister of José.** Illustrated by C. S. Reinhart. 12mo, $1.00.

Little Lord Fauntleroy. Sq. 8vo, $2.00. **Sara Crewe.** Sq. 8vo, $1.00. **Little Saint Elizabeth,** and Other Stories. 12mo, $1.50. Illustrated by R. B. Birch.

"Mrs. Burnett discovers gracious secrets in rough and forbidding natures—the sweetness that often underlies their bitterness—the soul of goodness in things evil. She seems to have an intuitive perception of character."—RICHARD HENRY STODDARD.

William Allen Butler.

Domesticus. A Tale of the Imperial City. 12mo, $1.25.

"Under a veil made intentionally transparent, the author maintains a running fire of good-natured hits at contemporary social follies."—*The New York Journal of Commerce.*

George W. Cable.

The Grandissimes. 12mo, paper, 50 cts.; cloth, $1.25. **Old Creole Days.** 12mo, cloth, $1.25; also in two parts, paper, each, 30 cts. **Dr. Sevier.** 12mo, paper, 50 cts.; cloth, $1.25. **Bonaventure.** 12mo, paper, 50 cts.; $1.25.

The set, 4 vols., $5.00.

"There are few living American writers who can reproduce for us more perfectly than Mr. Cable does, in his best moments, the speech, the manners, the whole social atmosphere of a remote time and a peculiar people. A delicious flavor of humor penetrates his stories."

—*The New York Tribune.*

Rebecca Harding Davis.

Silhouettes of American Life. 12mo, paper, 50 cts.; cloth, $1.00.

"There are altogether thirteen stories in the volume, all written in that direct, forcible style which is Mrs. Davis's distinctive merit as a producer of fiction."—*Boston Beacon.*

Richard Harding Davis.

Gallegher, and Other Stories. 12mo, paper, 50 cts. ; cloth, **$1.00.**

The ten stories comprising this volume attest the appearance of a new and strong individuality in the field of American fiction. They are of a wide range and deal with very varied types of metropolitan character and situation ; but each proves that Mr. Davis knows his New York as well as Dickens did his London.

Edward Eggleston.

Roxy. The Circuit Rider. Illustrated. Each, 12mo, $1.50.

"Dr. Eggleston's fresh and vivid portraiture of a phase of life and manners, hitherto almost unrepresented in literature ; its boldly contrasted characters, and its unconventional, hearty, religious spirit, took hold of the public imagination."—*The Christian Union.*

Erckmann-Chatrian.

The Conscript. Illustrated. **Waterloo.** Illustrated. Sequel to The Conscript. **Madame Thérèse. The Blockade of Phalsburg.** Illustrated. **The Invasion of France in 1814.** Illustrated. **A Miller's Story of the War.** Illustrated.

The National Novels, each, $1.25 ; the sets, 6 vol., $7.50.

Friend Fritz. 12mo, paper, 50 cts.; cloth, $1.25.

Eugene Field.

A Little Book of Profitable Tales. 16mo, $1.25.

"This pretty little volume promises to perpetuate examples of a wit, humor, and pathos quaint and rare in their kind."—*New York Tribune.*

Harold Frederic.

Seth's Brother's Wife. 12mo, $1.25. **The Lawton Girl.** 12mo, $1.25 ; paper, 50 cts. **In the Valley.** Illustrated. 12mo, $1.50.

"It is almost reasonable to assert that there has not been since Cooper's day a better American novel dealing with a purely historical theme than 'In the Valley.'"—*Boston Beacon.*

James Anthony Froude.

The Two Chiefs of Dunboy. An Irish Romance of the Last Century. 12mo, paper, 50 cts.; cloth, $1.50.

"The narrative is full of vigor, spirit and dramatic power. It will unquestionably be widely read, for it presents a vivid and life-like study of character with romantic color, and adventurous incident for the background."—*The New York Tribune.*

Robert Grant.

Face to Face. 12mo, paper, 50 cts.; cloth, $1.25. **The Reflections of a Married Man.** 12mo, paper, 50 cts.; cloth, $1.00.

"In the 'Reflections,' Mr. Grant has given us a capital little book which should easily strike up literary comradeship with 'The Reveries of a Bachelor.'" —*Boston Transcript.*

Edward Everett Hale.

Philip Nolan's Friends. Illust'd. 12mo, paper, 50 cts.; cloth, $1.50.

"There is no question, we think, that this is Mr. Hale's completest and best novel."—*The Atlantic Monthly.*

Marion Harland.

Judith. 12mo, paper, 50 cts.; cloth, $1.00. **Handicapped.** 12mo, $1.50. **With the Best Intentions.** 12mo, cloth, $1.00; paper, 50 cts.

"Fiction has afforded no more charming glimpses of old Virginia life than are found in this delightful story, with its quaint pictures, its admirably drawn characters, its wit, and its frankness."

—*The Brooklyn Daily Times.*

Joel Chandler Harris.

Free Joe, and Other Georgian Sketches. 12mo, paper, 50 cts.; cloth, $1.00.

"The author's skill as a story writer has never been more felicitously illustrated than in this volume."—*The New York Sun.*

Augustus Allen Hayes.

The Jesuit's Ring. 12mo, paper, 50 cts.; cloth, $1.00.

"The conception of the story is excellent."—*The Boston Traveller.*

George A. Hibbard.

The Governor, and Other Stories. 12mo, cloth, $1.00; paper, 50 cts.

"It is still often urged that, except in remote corners, there is nothing in our American life which appeals to the artistic sense, but certainly these stories are American to the core, and yet the artistic sense is strong in them throughout."—*Critic.*

E. T. W. Hoffmann.

Weird Tales. With Portrait. 12mo, 2 vols., $3.00.

"All those who are in search of a genuine literary sensation, or who care for the marvelous and supernatural, will find these two volumes fascinating reading."—*The Christian Union.*

Dr. J. G. Holland.

Sevenoaks. The Bay Path. Arthur Bonnicastle. Miss Gilbert's Career. Nicholas Minturn. Each, 12mo, $1.25; the set, $6.25. **Sevenoaks** and **Arthur Bonnicastle.** Each, paper, 50c.

"Dr. Holland will always find a congenial audience in the homes of culture and refinement. He does not affect the play of the darker and fiercer passions, but delights in the sweet images that cluster around the domestic hearth. He cherishes a strong fellow-feeling with the pure and tranquil life in the modest social circles of the American people, and has thus won his way to the companionship of many friendly hearts."
—*The New York Tribune.*

Thomas A. Janvier.

Color Studies, and a Mexican Campaign. 12mo, paper, 50 cts.; cloth, $1.00.

"Piquant, novel and ingenious, these little stories, with all their simplicity, have excited a wide interest. The best of them, 'Jaune D'Antimoine,' is a little wonder in its dramatic effect, its ingenious construction."—*Critic.*

Andrew Lang.

The Mark of Cain. 12mo, paper, 25 cts.

"No one can deny that it is crammed as full of incident as it will hold, or that the elaborate plot is worked out with most ingenious perspicuity."
—*The Saturday Review.*

George P. Lathrop.

Newport. 12mo, paper, 50 cts.; cloth, $1.25. **An Echo of Passion.** 12mo, paper, 50 cts.; cloth, $1.00. **In the Distance.** 12mo, paper, 50 cts.; cloth, $1.00.

"His novels have the refinement of motive which characterize the analytical school, but his manner is far more direct and dramatic."
—*The Christian Union.*

Brander Matthews.

The Secret of the Sea, and Other Stories. 12mo, paper, 50 cts.; cloth, $1.00. **The Last Meeting.** 12mo, cloth, $1.00.

"Mr. Matthews is a man of wide observation and of much familiarity with the world. His literary style is bright and crisp, with a peculiar sparkle about it—wit and humor judiciously mingled—which renders his pages more than ordinarily interesting."—*The Rochester Post-Express.*

George Moore.

Vain Fortune. 12mo, $1.00.

"How a woman's previous ideas and actions will completely change when the medium of a wild, intense love is interposed, was never more skilfully sketched."—*Boston Times.*

Fitz-James O'Brien.

The Diamond Lens, with Other Stories. 12mo, paper, 50 cts.

"These stories are the only things in literature to be compared with Poe's work, and if they do not equal it in workmanship, they certainly do not yield to it in originality."—*The Philadelphia Record.*

Duffield Osborne.

The Spell of Ashtaroth. 12mo, $1.00.

"It has a simple but picturesque plot, and the story is told in a vividly dramatic way."—*Chicago Times.*

Bliss Perry.

The Broughton House. 12mo, $1.25.

"A wonderfully shrewd and vivid picture of life in one of our hill towns in summer."—*Hartford Post.*

Thomas Nelson Page.

In Old Virginia. Marse Chan and Other Stories. 12mo, $1.25. **On Newfound River.** 12mo, $1.00. **Elsket,** and Other Stories. 12mo, $1.00. **Marse Chan.** Ills. by Smedley. Sq. 12mo. $1.50.

"Mr. Page enjoys the distinction of having written the most exquisite story of the war ('Marse Chan'), which has yet appeared. His stories are beautiful and faithful pictures of a society now become a portion and parcel of the irrevocable past."—*Harper's Magazine.*

George I. Putnam.

In Blue Uniform. 12mo, $1.00.

The author of this love story, who is an ex-army officer, has given a very natural picture of garrison life in the Far West, with strong character studies, and a sufficient diversity of incident to give movement and cumulative interest to the tale.

Saxe Holm's Stories.

First Series. Second Series. Each, 12mo, paper, 50c; cloth, $1.00.

"Saxe Holm's characters are strongly drawn, and she goes right to the heart of human experience, as one who knows the way. We heartily commend them as vigorous, wholesome, and sufficiently exciting stories."

—*The Advance.*

Stories from Scribner.

Stories of New York. Illustrated. From Four to Six, by Annie Eliot; The Commonest Possible Story, by Bliss Perry; The End of the Beginning, by George A. Hibbard; A Puritan Ingénue, by John S. Wood; Mrs. Manstey's View, by Edith Wharton.

Stories of the Railway. Illustrated. As the Sparks Fly Upward, by George A. Hibbard; How I Sent My Aunt to Baltimore, by Charles S. Davison; Run to Seed, by Thomas Nelson Page; Flandroe's Mogul, by A. C. Gordon.

In Press: **Stories of the South.** **Stories of Italy.** **Stories of the Sea.** **Stories of the Army.**

Illustrated. Each, 16mo, paper, 50 cts.; cloth, 75 cts.; half calf, $1.50.

The stories in these attractive little volumes are among the most popular of those that have been published in "Scribner's Magazine." They are daintily bound, and fully and beautifully illustrated.

Robert Louis Stevenson.

Strange Case of Dr. Jekyll and Mr. Hyde. 12mo, paper, 25 cts.; cloth, $1.00. **Kidnapped.** 12mo, paper, 50 cts.; cloth, ill., $1.25. **The Merry Men,** and Other Tales and Fables. 12mo, paper, 35 cts.; cloth, $1.00. **New Arabian Nights.** 12mo, paper, 30 cts.; cloth, $1.00. **The Dynamiter.** 12mo, paper, 30 cts.; cloth, $1.00. **The Black Arrow.** Ill. 12mo, paper, 50 cts.; cloth, $1.00. **The Wrong Box.** 12mo, paper, 50 cts.; cloth, $1.00. **The Master of Ballantrae.** 12mo, paper, 50 cts.; cloth, ill., $1.25. **The Wrecker.** 12mo, ill., $1.25. **Island Nights' Entertainments.** 12mo, ill., $1.25.

"Stevenson belongs to the romantic school of fiction writers. He is original in style, charming, fascinating, and delicious, with a marvelous command of words, and with a manner ever delightful and magnetic."
—*Boston Transcript.*

Charles Warren Stoddard.

South Sea Idyls. 12mo, $1.50.

"Brimful of delicious descriptions of South Sea Island life. Neither Loti nor Stevenson has expressed from tropical life the luscious, fruity delicacy, or the rich wine-like bouquet of these sketches."—*Independent.*

T. R. Sullivan.

Day and Night Stories. First and Second Series. Each, 12mo, cloth, $1.00; paper, 50 cts. **Roses of Shadow.** 12mo, $1.00.

"Mr. Sullivan's style is at once easy and refined, conveying most happily that atmosphere of good breeding and polite society which is indispensable to the novel of manners, but which so many of them lamentably fail of."—*The Nation.*

Frederick J. Stimson (J. S. of Dale).

Guerndale. 12mo, paper, 50 cts.; cloth, $1.25. **The Crime of Henry Vane.** 12mo, paper, 50 cts.; cloth, $1.00. **The Sentimental Calendar.** Ill. 12mo, $1.00. **First Harvest.** 12mo, $1.25. **The Residuary Legatee.** 12mo, paper, 35 cts.; cloth, $1.00. **In the Three Zones.** 12mo, $1.00.

"No young novelist in this country seems better equipped than Mr. Stimson is."—*The Philadelphia Bulletin.*

Frank R. Stockton.

Rudder Grange. 12mo, paper, 60 cts.; cloth, $1.25; illustrated by A. B. Frost, Sq. 12mo, $2.00. **The Late Mrs. Null.** 12mo, paper, 50 cts.; cloth, $1.25. **The Lady, or The Tiger?** and Other Stories. 12mo, paper, 50 cts.; cloth, $1.25. **The Christmas Wreck,** and Other Stories. 12mo, paper, 50 cts.; cloth, $1.25. **The Bee-Man of Orn,** and Other Fanciful Tales. 12mo, cloth, $1.25. **Amos Kilbright,** with Other Stories. 12mo, paper, 50 cts.; cloth, $1.25. **The Rudder Grangers Abroad,** and Other Stories. 12mo, paper, 50 cts.; cloth, $1.25.

"Of Mr. Stockton's stories what is there to say, but that they are an unmixed blessing and delight? He is surely one of the most inventive of talents, discovering not only a new kind in humor and fancy, but accumulating an inexhaustible wealth of details in each fresh achievement, the least of which would be riches from another hand."—W. D. Howells.

Stories by American Authors.

Cloth, 16mo, 50 cts. each; set, 10 vols., $5.00; cabinet edition, in sets only, $7.50.

"The public ought to appreciate the value of this series, which is preserving permanently in American literature short stories that have contributed to its advancement."—*The Boston Globe.*

Octave Thanet.

Expiation. Illustrated by A. B. Frost. 12mo, paper, 50 cts.; cloth, $1.00. **Stories of a Western Town.** 12mo. Illustrated by A. B. Frost. $1.25.

Octave Thanet has in this new book of Western stories a completely fresh field, in which she has done her finest work. These stories portray the types and conditions of life in the thriving, pushing towns of the great Central Western States with knowledge, sympathy and a fine literary art.

John T. Wheelwright.

A Child of the Century. 12mo, paper, 50 cts.; cloth, $1.00.

"A typical story of political and social life, free from cynicism of morbid realism, and brimming over with fun."—*The Christian at Work.*

www.ingramcontent.com/pod-product-compliance
Lightning Source LLC
Chambersburg PA
CBHW030404270326
41926CB00009B/1262

* 9 7 8 3 3 3 7 0 0 4 7 0 5 *